Hack The World with OSINT

Chris Kubecka

Hack the World with OSINT

Published by Chris Kubecka & HypaSec

HypaSec is a registered entity in the Netherlands Commercial Registration: 63945517

Printed in the Netherlands
First Printing
ISBN: 978-0-9956875-9-2

Publisher: HypaSec, Netherlands
Graphics: Chris Kubecka
Technical Editor: E. Martinez II
Indexer: Chris Kubecka

British Library Cataloguing-in-Publication Data

This book is written in British International English not US English

Application Submitted

Why a IT/IOT/ICS hacking book?

Nice people don't connect exploitable systems to the internet.
- Random Twitter User

Censys has been an invaluable tool in my OSINT toolbox. As such, I chose to share the knowledge, prompting me to write down the ins and outs of how to use the free tool with examples and case studies. Censys was very useful in the creation of a penetration course I wrote and taught at BSides Las Vegas in 2017. Although I love Shodan, Censys pulled me in with a different type of searching and discovery of interesting or weak systems. Shodan, becoming more and more my device OSINT side chic so to speak.

Table of Contents

Where was that figure?

Where was that table?

Why Censys rocks!

0.1 Introduction

Open source intelligence gathering (OSINT) and web-based reconnaissance is an integral part of penetration testing and proactive defence. The more connected we are, the more information is held about everything. Yummy, juicy information for both a penetration tester or a malicious actor. Learning what sources of are available to start your search is an essential first step in learning about reconnaissance and how the information could be utilised or resold. Both issues you or your client need to know. All of the tools and techniques in this book can be ninjafied with Python, SQL, SDK or PowerShell.

0.2 Target Audience

Penetration testers, security and network analysis or anyone curious about open source intelligence gathering. Defenders and exploiters alike.

0.3 Conventions

Sensitive information may be removed from the examples, or modified.

0.4 Other Resources

Tools which can use all or part of Censys.io and ZMap

Tool name	URL
Python	**www.python.org/downloads/**
Censys web search	**Censys.io**

ZMap & tools	**github.com/zmap/zmap**
Recon NG	**bitbucket.org/LaNMaSteR53/recon-ng**
Maltego	**www.paterva.com/web7/**
Spiderfoot	**www.spiderfoot.net/**
Metasploit	**www.metasploit.com/**
NMap	**nmap.org/**
PowerShell	**docs.microsoft.com/en-us/powershell/scripting/powershell-scripting?view=powershell-6**

0.5 Request for Comments

Bugs@hypasec.com

0.6 Acknowledgements

My significant other, who was patient and supportive through my grumbles, gripes and cursing at Word whilst writing this book. Friends Colonel JC Vega, LanaSec my sane lady rock, M. Blackmeer, @Marmusha chemical mayhem, stage shy former military intelligence, Commander Tosh, Jeff Man, David Z & Olga, Dr. Anita D'Amico & CodeDx, Joe Gray, Security BSides Amsterdam, London and LV crew, Caroline Wong, OWASP OC, Jack Rhysider Darknet Diaries, Austrian EU Presidency and Energy CERT, Dr./Lawyer/Diplomat Lucy, APPG AI, IoActive & Jennifer Sunshine, NSA, FBI Dr. WiFi, Andy Yen/ Proton Mail, evil gamemaster brother from another mother Stefan, Drew J and all the happy hackers out there who helped support me during the research and writing of this book.

0.7 Technology and tools to create the book

- VMWare Workstation Pro 12 and 14
- Two Asus ROG laptops, sadly one broke writing this book, the other is called Zombie
- Python & PowerShell

- Kali Penetration Testing Operating System
- (I hate) Word
- Mc Frontalot & YT Cracker's music

0.8 Protocol References

Censys is based on the ZMap project. ZMap is capable of multiple protocols; however, its capable of NTP but does not utilize the protocol fully.

Table 1 Zmap and Censys.io protocols

Protocol name	Default port
BACnet	47808
CWMP	7547
DNP3	20000
DNS	53
FTP	21
HTTP	80
HTTPS	443
IMAP	143
IMAPS	993
MODBUS	502
NTP	123
Niagara Fox	1911
POP3	25
POP3S	995

Siemens S7	102
SMTP	25
SMTPS	465
SSH	22
UPnP	1900

0.9 Organization of the book

The book is divided by major protocol and service. Examples for each service and risk importance in a penetration and security researcher perspective.

Chapter 1: The Censys.io and ZMap.io Project
Information about the two projects and usefulness

Chapter 2: Setting up your OSINT lab
Get your virtual machine, lab and tools prepared. with API keys.

Chapter 3: Remote Management
FTP, SSH and Telnet protocols.

Chapter 4: Email
SMTP, SMTPS, IMAP, IMAPS, POP3 and POP3S

Chapter 5: HTTP & HTTPS
Web services over HTTP and HTTPS

Chapter 6: Dorking with Censys
Search engines are your friend: they want to help you find juicy files and vulnerable systems.

Chapter 7: ICS & Scada
BACnet, Fox, DNP3, MODBUS and Siemens S7

Chapter 8: Building Control Systems & IoT
Search engines are your friend: they want to help you find building

control systems and the Internet of Sh*t vulnerable systems.

Chapter 9: Other Protocols
DNS, UPnP, SMB

Chapter 10: Tags
How to leverage labelling performed by Censys called Tags.

Chapter 11: Reports
Detailed reports, pinpointing vulnerable or hacked systems and more.

Chapter 12: Censys with Tools
Combine the Censys API with some of your favourite hacking tools like Metasploit and Recon NG.

Chapter 13: Rest API
Using Censys to its fullest extent is the Rest API.

Companion Website
The companion website for the book is at, at **https://tools.hypasec.com/.** Here you will find downloads, URL links, tips and tricks and any errata.

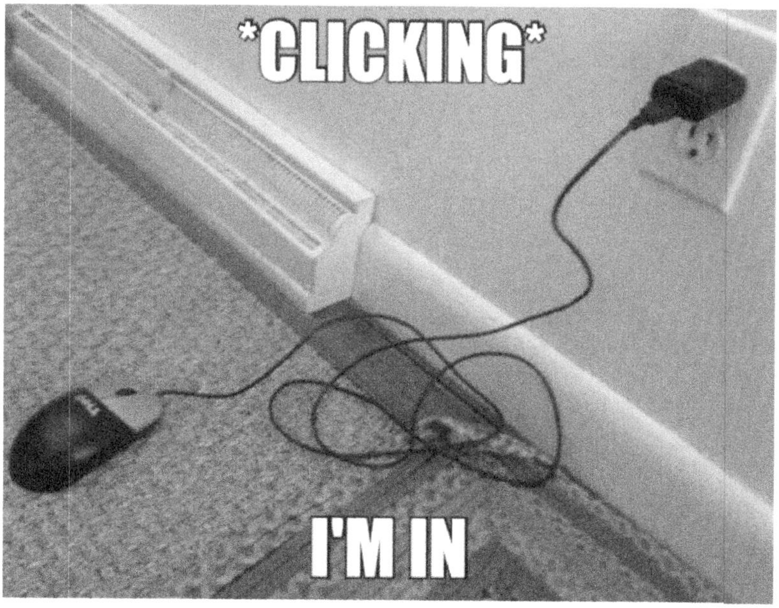

Chapter 1

The Censys & ZMap Projects

INFORMATION IN THIS CHAPTER:

- What Censys is and why it's useful
- ZMap
- ZTag

Give me two hours to setup my attack machine and I can become the master of the internet.

- Abraham Lincoln

1 What is Censys

1.1 Introduction to Censys

A web, API and SQL interactive project from the University of Michigan, USA. It allows searching, like Googling but instead of website content, asset information on specific ports. Security researchers can ask questions concerning the devices or networks on the internet. Several tools such as ZMap are the backbone of Censys. Reporting is available, accessible to use and well documented. Currently, access is free, but there are data and SQL limitations with some types of services only available to verified researchers and academic accounts. Censys leverages ZMap and multiple ZMap related projects.

Censys.io performs weekly scans of the IPv4 internet address space.

That data is transparently stored in an accessible database. After Censys processes and parses the data into human and extensible annotation framework format, allowing programmable interaction. Once researchers discover devices, they are encouraged to contribute by additionally scanning for more protocols and to annotate findings by devices or properties.

In real life, attackers can spend anywhere from 80%-90% of their time in the reconnaissance part of their attack; penetration testing is not that much different. Perhaps the client wants to know mainly IT, IoT or ICS vulnerabilities. Some need to know much more about their public exposure and internet exposed assets. If an organisation is proactive in its defence, OSINT is crucial.

DefCon, the largest hacker conference in the USA, held yearly in Las Vegas, holds many different contests. One of these contests is the Social Engineering World Championship. At DefCon 22, I copied down some of the flags and points associated with them.

Table 2 Common Social Engineering competition points/flags

Information	Points
Any undisclosed or orphan subdomains?	10
Untrusted or weak encryption certificates?	6
Does the target expose internal network or asset information?	8
Is there a VPN and is it configured?	8
Any general misconfigurations?	10
Any IoT exposed on the internet?	6
Any ICS exposed on the internet?	10
Any remoting tools exposed to the internet?	10

What operating system version is in use?	10
Any Wi-Fi in use?	4
Any sensitive services exposed?	6
Any third party weak configurations or exposure?	8
Any indications of compromise past or present?	25

Censys will banner grab, try to name services and ports running on a system or website. Censys will return:

- ☑ A summary page of the IP address
- ☑ Google maps
- ☑ Ports open
- ☑ Certificate information
- ☑ Checks for the Heartbleed vulnerability
- ☑ Banner grabs
- ☑ Performs a StartTLS initiation

1.2 Censys Protocols

Censys scans multiple protocols and ports, but not every single one. There are also ports and protocols which are scanned but no longer reported publicly or some scans were cancelled because they discovered way too much bad stuff on the internet. If you are in need of these and other ports and protocols, you can install ZMap and the family of tools and scan the internet using the tools.

Table 3 Censys.io and ZMap Protocols

Protocol	Description
BACNET	Industrial control system protocol
CWMP	CPE WAN Management Protocol
DNP3	Industrial control system protocol
DNS	Domain Naming Services

FOX	Building automation protocol
FTP	File Transport Protocol
HTTP	Hyper Text Transport Protocol & Web Services
IMAP	Internet Message Access Protocol
MODBUS	Industrial control system protocol
NTP*	Network Time Protocol, ***Censys.io does not scan this protocol***
POP3	Post Office Protocol
S7	Siemens S7 Industrial control system protocol
SMB	Server Message Block
SMTP	Simple Mail Transport Protocol
SSH	Secure Shell
SSLV2	Secure Socket Layer version 2
TELNET	Bi-directional text-oriented communication and control
UPNP	Universal Plug and Play

Further, detailed information can be found on the project GitHub: **https://github.com/zmap/ztag/tree/master/ztag/transforms**

1.3 Censys Query Syntax

Censys goes the extra mile, trying to be a researcher and commercial resource, with a low learning curve. Additional query examples are available at Censys:

https://censys.io/ipv4/help?q=&collection=

Table 4 Censys.io query syntax examples

Query Syntax	Example
General keyword search	Hacked
Specific fields	80.http.get.status_code: 418
Boolean Logic	And, or, not By default all terms are treated as optional or statement
Networks	ip:53.20.0.0/14 ip:[199.0.0.100 TO 199.0.0.210]
Host names	10
Protocols	Protocols: "502/modbus"
In-line DNS queries	a:cnn.com mx:spamalot.com
Ranges	(25.smtp.starttls.starttls) AND 25.smtp.starttls.starttls: [4.1.0 TO 4.3.5]
Wildcards	10
Regular expressions	Standard Regex expressions
Boosting	Using the ^ character can make one term more important than another when searching
Reserved characters	There are 22 reserved characters + Logical **Addition** operator

- Logical **Subtraction** operator

= Logical **Equals** operator

& Logical **AND** operator

| | Logical **OR** operator

> Logical **Greater than** operator

< Logical **Less than** operator

! Logical **Not equal to** operator

(

)

{ Open bracket for **exclusive ranges**

} Closed bracket for **exclusive ranges**

[Open bracket for **inclusive ranges**

] Closed bracket for **inclusive ranges**

^ Carat for **boosting**

“

~

*

?

:

\

/

1.4 Censys Web Query examples

There are three separate containers of information on Censys. Each one is used for different searches and discovering different types of information. However, reporting and web searching can merge the three in exciting ways. Web examples are available with test searching at:

https://censys.io/ipv4/help/examples?q=&collection=

- IPv4 Hosts
- Websites
- Certificates

Table 5 Censys Example Web Search Queries

Search Query	Example Results
tags.raw: "http"	IPv4 Hosts running the HTTP protocol
protocols.raw: "443/https"	IPv4 Hosts running the HTTPS protocol
(tags.raw: "http") AND protocols.raw: "22/ssh"	IPv4 Hosts running the HTTP protocol AND the SSH Protocol
autonomous_system.description.raw: "DIGITALOCEAN-ASN - DigitalOcean, LLC, US"	IPv4 Any autonomous system belonging to the Digital Ocean network
80.http.get.body: "DVR Components Download"	IPv4 All web pages which in the HTTP Body have DVR Components Download
FTP	**protocols.raw: "21/ftp"**
HTTP	**protocols.raw: "80/http"**

References

The creators of Censys.io and the ZMAP project wrote an academic paper explaining the researcher value and speed of internet scanning.

Censys paper **https://censys.io/static/censys.pdf**

@InProceedings{censys15, author = {Zakir Durumeric and David Adrian and Ariana Mirian and Michael Bailey and J. Alex Halderman}, title = {A Search Engine Backed by {I}nternet-Wide Scanning}, booktitle = {Proceedings of the 22nd ACM Conference on Computer and Communications Security}, month = oct, year = 2015 }

https://censys.io/overview

https://censys.io/about

GeoLocation services are provided using the MaxMind GeoLite2 database unless specified otherwise. Routing information is provided by Merit Network and Team Cymru.
http://www.maxmind.com/

Chapter 2

Getting your tools ready

INFORMATION IN THIS CHAPTER:

- OSINT lab environment
- Setting up Censys account
- Obtaining API key & Secret
- Setting up VM/Kali
- Installing Maltego, Censys Python library, ZMap & Recon NG

By failing to prepare, you are preparing to fail.

- Benjamin Franklin

2 How to Setup your OSINT Lab

There are some essential tools required to set up your OSINT lab. They aren't too complicated and shouldn't cost any additional money. Some of the tools do have commercial versions. If you download anything, check the hash MD5 + SHA-1 or SHA-2 256 or above. MD5 is too short, so should not be relied on solely. Also, check files with anti-virus or Virustotal.com. Be safe when setting up your lab. Another way to keep safe, using virtualisation and sandboxes. If you are introducing your testing machine into a client environment, don't infect the customer.

Penetration testing machines are only that, for penetration testing. Be aware, out of the box; Kali isn't configured securely. They are setup to test other machines, not to be tested. There are modules in Kali tools that can attack other Kali machines. Keep that in mind when setting up and securing your lab. Don't check your online banking, get sensitive data off, harden where possible.

2.1 Lab requirements

- ☑ A good, fast, relatively uncensored internet connection.
- ☑ A computer with at least 2GB extra RAM to dedicate to Kali and other tools
- ☑ If you use Kali, a computer that can run it with some basic Linux knowledge
- ☑ You may need to install additional tools
    - o VM Player or Workstation Pro version 14 & above
    - o Book OSINT VM or Kali Linux 64 bit based image
    - o Censys Python library
    - o ZMap
- ☑ A Censys.io account API Key and API Secret
- ☑ Censys API Keys and accounts for Recon NG
- ☑ Censys API Keys and accounts for Maltego

Using the OSINT Kali Distribution, a custom distribution built from Kali. Is by far, the easiest way to setup your lab. It already has Censys Python library and ZMap installed; as well as, all the regular 300+ installed Kali tools.

If you want or need to setup your lab from scratch. Offensive Security, the company behind Kali have many different types of Kali images. You can run in a Live configuration, ARM, VM, Hyper-V, Raspberry Pi, etc. Kali comes with Nmap and Maltego Community Edition (CE) but Censys Python library and ZMap for some of the exercises.

If you don't want to use Linux at all. The tools and labs can be run on a Windows based machine, version 7 or higher. You would need to install Python, Maltego Metasploit and ZMap. Recon NG runs on Linux only.

2.2 OSINT Kali Distribution Information

The book OSINT Kali distribution is available from the companion website: **https://tools.hypasec.com** or the listed Torrent. It is built on the standard 2017.1 version of Kali from Offensive Security but updated and customized. The book distribution has the following features:

- The network on Ethernet, which is eth0 is DHCP. You can change this if required for your network. This can change depending on your configuration.
- Firefox web browser
- Metasploit
- Maltego
- OWASP ZAP 2.70
- VMWare 14 compatible
- 2GB RAM, 2 Processors 2 Cores
- 40 GB hard drive
- Network is Bridged

2.3 OSINT Kali64 in WM Player/Workstation/Fusion 14

Using the book OSINT Kali distribution is the easiest way to begin. This version is for version 12 of VM Ware. It uses the proprietary format of VM Ware.

Open VMWare Player, Fusion or Workstation 12. It will bring up a welcome page. On the welcome page, chose **Open a Virtual Machine**. Browse to the folder where you the extracted image. Open the **Clone of OSINTKali64.vmx** fil. VM Ware will import the virtual machine. Press the **Play virtual machine** button. The Kali machine will open. When prompted, enter the username and password to log in as root.

Username: **root** Password: **Lamarr**

2.4 OSINT Kali64 OVF in VM Player/Workstation 14

OVF is an exportable format with OpenBox and VMWare compatibility. There are some caveats: OVF can act oddly sometimes for no known reason after conversion. To be on the safe side, make copies, snapshots, and backup as required.

Open VMWare Player, Fusion or Workstation 14. It will bring up a welcome page. On the welcome page, chose **Open a Virtual Machine**. Browse to the folder where you the extracted image. A Pop-up box will appear, Keep or change the name, then pick a Storage path for the new virtual machine. Click the **Import** button.

You will probably get another pop-up warning/error which tells you:

The import failed because it didn't meet the hardware specification… Press the **Retry** button. Your machine will import in a few minutes. Press the **Play virtual machine** button

Username: **root** Password: **Lamarr**

2.4 Installing and updating tools

Installing the tools on Kali is easy. Download the Kali image which fits your needs at the Offensive Security website **https://www.offensive-security.com/kali-linux-vmware-virtualbox-image-download/**. Install following the Offensive Security directions. Next, install the OSINT tools. If you chose Windows, not all the tools will work. However, some do come in Windows and are easy to setup but can require Python. To install ZMap on Kali, you will need to add the Debian package repository to your list of repositories or download all the dependencies and compile ZMap.

Tool	Type in bold as root # to install/upgrade
Upgrading Maltego CE	Open Maltego from Applications| Information Gathering |Maltego After opening Maltego and go to Investigate |Tools |
Install ZMap	# apt-get install zmap
Update Metasploit	# service postgresql start # msfconsole msf> msfupdate msf> exit # msfconsole
Censys Python Library	# pip install censys
Install Recon NG	apt-get update && apt-get install recon-ng

2.5 Installing Maltego on Windows

1. Download Maltego at **https://www.paterva.com/web7/downloads.php**
2. Unzip
3. Install in a folder of your choice

4. Run the EXE to install and start

2.6 Email Account Helper Tool 10-Minute Email

Before creating new accounts and registering. Since this is a lab environment, use more anonymous, temporary email account. There are many websites which offer this free service. You get a temporary email account good for 10 minutes or more to register for API keys and vendor accounts. Most of the temporary email providers are not secure, so don't use the temporary email account for anything personal or vital.

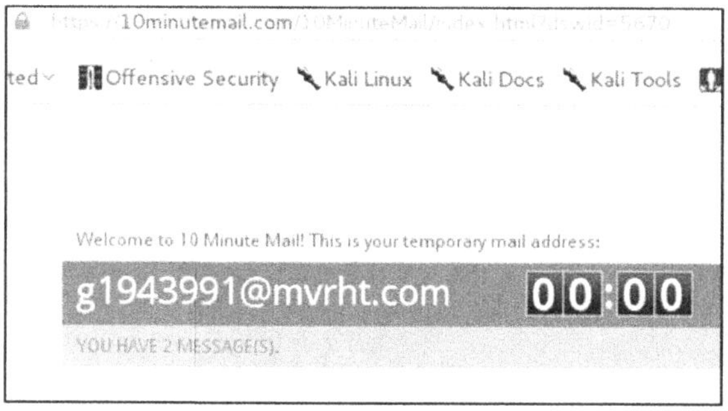

Figure 1 10-Minute temporary email account

10-Minute email or other variants. They come in many languages. There is 20-minute email, 30-minute, etc. Put 10-minute email in a search engine and utilize to setup your lab accounts.

2.7 Obtaining API Keys

To search databases effectively on the internet, you need API keys. You will need to setup some accounts to get API keys, using 10-minute email or similar.

Censys.io API Key and Secret

1. Go to **http://www.censys.io**
2. Sign up and log in
3. Click **My Account**
4. Your API key and Secret are in API Credentials

2.8 Configuring Maltego and API Keys

Setting up Maltego for Windows, OSINT Kali and Kali is the same. Register for a Maltego account at:

https://www.paterva.com/web7/community/community.php

1. Get your Censys API Keys ready
2. Open Maltego
3. Register for an account or sign-in
4. You will enable all but one transform:

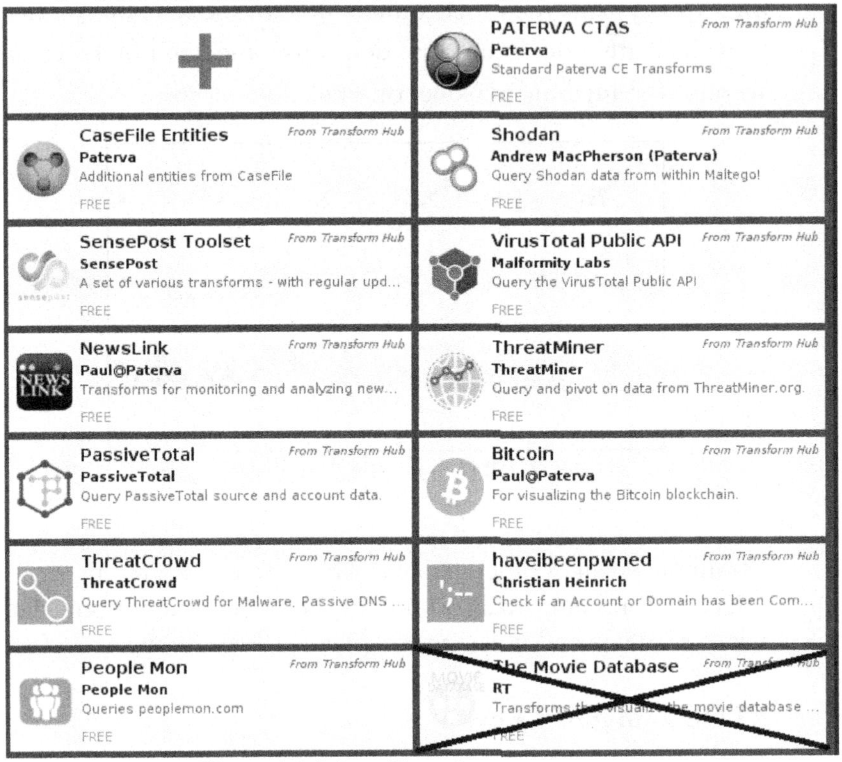

Figure 2 Maltego Transform options

5. For all the transforms but The Movie Database. Hover over the transform, click **Install**, **Yes**, then **Finish**.
6. For the **Censys** transform. Hover over, click the Settings button, then enter the API keys, then click close.

Figure 3 Maltego Transform seed settings

Now you are all setup. Sit back, relax, have a glass of something you like to drink and feel good. Your OSINT environment setup is finished! Happy hacker face☺

References

Table 6 Tool URL reference

Name	URL Location
OSINT-Kali Distribution	https://tools.hypasec.com/
Official Kali	https://www.offensive-security.com/kali-linux-vmware-virtualbox-image-download/
Censys Python Library	https://github.com/censys/censys-python
Maltego	https://www.paterva.com/web7/downloads.php https://github.com/mpars0ns/maltego_censys

HypaSec Tools	https://hypasec.com/tools
ZMap	https://zmap.io
ZGrab	https://github.com/zmap/zgrab
Go Language	https://golang.org/dl/

Chapter 3

FTP, SSH and Telnet

INFORMATION IN THIS CHAPTER:

- Using Censys to survey remote management protocols
- Discovering specific configurations
- Specific vendor discovery via protocol dorking
- Finding vulnerable systems

When the internet gives you remotely exploitable systems, take them. They're like free samples, right?

- Chris Kubecka

3 Remote Management

3.1 Introduction to Censys Remote Management Protocols

Remote management of computers, servers, devices like printers or network equipment is quite common on intranets and the internet. High speed bandwidth and other advances have enabled more systems connected to the internet, bringing functionality and convenience. However, security is usually an afterthought.

Some of the major protocols in use are FTP, SSH and Telnet. There is a secure version of FTP called SFTP but Telnet is not a secure protocol. Contrary to the Telnet Wikipedia article statement "SSH has practically replaced Telnet, and the older protocol is used these days only in rare cases to access decades old legacy equipment that does not support more modern protocols." An internet scan by ZMap, reported by Censys, shows Telnet is still in widespread use, about half as much as SSH on over four million systems.

Table 7 Censys Remote management protocols

Protocol	Number	Percentage
FTP	10,478,747	4.79%
SSH	9,821,332	4.49%
TELNET	4,332,915	1.98%
Total	24,632,994	11.26%

Table 8 Censys Remote management tags

Protocol	Number	Percentage
IDRAC	10,247	0.0%
IPMI	75,472	0.03%
FTP	10,478,747	4.79%
Remote access	7,653	0.0%
Total	10,572,119	4.82%

3.2 Exploring FTP services

Details, settings and configurations of the FTP protocol which can be used in detailed searches.

Table 9 Important FTP Censys fields & examples

Censys field	Example
21.ftp.banner.banner	220-FileZilla Server 0.9.57 beta 220-written by Tim Kosse (tim.kosse@filezilla-project.org) 220 Please visit https://filezilla-project.org/
21.ftp.banner.metadata.description	FileZilla 0.9.57
21.ftp.banner.metadata.product	FileZilla
21.ftp.banner.metadata.version	0.9.57
21.ftp.banner.metadata.revision	Build 2

Table 10 FTP 1st digit server return codes

FTP Range	Description
1xx	Positive Preliminary reply
2xx	Positive Completion reply
3xx	Positive Intermediate reply
4xx	Transient Negative Completion reply

5xx	Permanent Negative Completion reply
6xx	Protected reply

Table 11 FTP 2nd digit codes

FTP Range	Description
x0x	Syntax
x1x	Information
x2x	Connections
x3x	Authentication and accounting
x4x	Unspecified
x5x	File system

Table 12 FTP 100 Series Codes

FTP Range	Description
100	The requested action is being initiated, expect another reply before proceeding with a new command.
110	Restart marker replay
120	Service ready in nnn minutes or Server Busy
125	Data connection already open; transfer starting
150	File status okay; about to open data connection

3.3 Finding FTP servers busy status

To find servers with this FTP setting: Code 120. Use the Censys web search function using the search string:

21.ftp.banner.banner: 120

Figure 4 FTP Code 120 Search

Table 13 FTP 200 Series Codes

FTP Range	Description
200	The requested action has been successfully completed
202	Command not implemented, superfluous at this site
211	System status, or system help reply
212	Directory status
213	File status
214	Help message
215	NAME system type
220	Service ready for new user
221	Service closing control connection
225	Data connection open; no transfer in progress

226	Closing data connection. Requested file action successful
227	Entering Passive Mode (h1,h2,h3,h4,p1,p2)
228	Entering Long Passive Mode (long address, port)
229	Entering Extended Passive Mode (|||port|)
230	User logged in, proceed. Logged out if appropriate
231	User logged out; service terminated
232	Logout command noted, will complete when transfer done
234	Specifies that the server accepts the authentication mechanism specified by the client, and the exchange of security data is complete (Microsoft)
250	Requested file action okay, completed
257	"PATHNAME" created

3.4 Finding FTP servers with user already logged in

To find servers with this FTP setting: Code 230. Use the Censys web search function using the search string, then click into the details on one on the systems:

21.ftp.banner.banner: 230

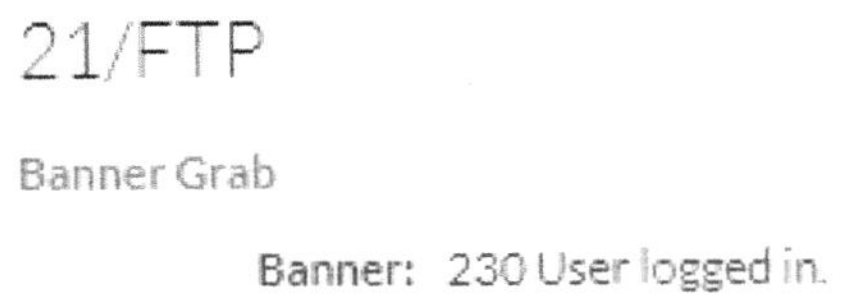

Figure 5 Details of a system with FTP Code 230

3.5 Finding FTP service banners

To find servers displaying an FTP service banner: Code 220. Use the Censys web search function using the search string. It will return both normal and oddly customized service names.

21.ftp.banner.banner: 220

Figure 6 Details of a system with FTP Code 220

Table 14 FTP 300 Series Codes

FTP Range	Description
300	The command has been accepted, but the requested action is on hold, pending receipt of further information
331	User name okay, need password
332	Need account for login or ThinServer
350	Requested file action pending further information

3.6 Finding FTP ThinServer

To find servers with this FTP setting: Code 332. Use the Censys web search function using the search string:

21.ftp.banner.banner: 332 AND 21.ftp.banner.banner: ThinServer

Figure 7 Details of a system with FTP Code 332

Table 15 FTP 400 Series Codes

FTP Range	Description
400	The command was not accepted and the requested action did not take place, but the error condition is temporary and the action may be requested again
421	Service not available, closing control connection
425	Can't open data connection
426	Connection closed; transfer aborted
430	Invalid username or password
434	Requested host unavailable
450	Requested file action not taken
451	Requested action aborted. Local error in processing
452	Requested action not taken. Insufficient storage space in system. File unavailable

3.7 Finding FTP MikroTik

To find servers with this FTP setting: Code 452. Use the Censys web search function using the search string:

21.ftp.banner.banner: 452 AND 21.ftp.banner.banner: MikroTik

Figure 8 Details of a system with FTP Code 452

Table 16 FTP 500 Series Codes

FTP Range	Description
500	Syntax error, command unrecognized and the requested action did not take place
501	Syntax error in parameters or arguments
502	Command not implemented
503	Bad sequence of commands
504	Command not implemented for that parameter
530	Not logged in
532	Need account for storing files
534	Could Not Connect to Server - Policy Requires SSL
550	Requested action not taken. File unavailable
551	Requested action aborted. Page type unknown
552	Requested file action aborted. Exceeded storage allocation
553	Requested action not taken. File name not allowed

3.8 Finding FTP syntax error

To find servers with this FTP setting: Code 500. Use the Censys web search function using the search string, then click one of the systems and look at the FTP details:

21.ftp.banner.banner: 500

Figure 9 Details of a system with FTP Code 500

Table 17 FTP 600 Series Codes

FTP Range	Description
600	Replies regarding confidentiality and integrity
631	Integrity protected reply
632	Confidentiality and integrity protected reply
633	Confidentiality protected reply

Table 18 FTP 10000 Series Codes

FTP Range	Description
10000	Common Winsock Error Codes

10054	Connection reset by peer. The connection was forcibly closed by the remote host
10060	Cannot connect to remote server
10061	Cannot connect to remote server. The connection is actively refused by the server
10066	Directory not empty
10068	Too many users, server is full

3.10 Exploring SSH services

Censys recognises the SSH protocol version 2 in its scans.

Table 19 Important SSH Censys fields & examples

Censys field	Example
22.ssh.v2.banner.comment	Ubuntu-2ubuntu2.3
22.ssh.v2.banner.raw	SSH-2.0-OpenSSH_6.6.1p1 Ubuntu-2ubuntu2.3
22.ssh.v2.banner.software	OpenSSH_6.6.1p1
22.ssh.v2.banner.version	2.0
22.ssh.v2.metadata.description	OpenSSH 6.6.1p1
22.ssh.v2.metadata.product	OpenSSH
22.ssh.v2.metadata.version	6.6.1p1
22.ssh.v2.selected.client_to_server.cipher	aes128-ctr
22.ssh.v2.selected.client_to_serve	none

r.compression	
22.ssh.v2.server_host_key.fingerprint_sha256	3123bf1a945f50a03ab7a80a415e0157cad51a9d7ce2e7317e7b7480f1d817fc
22.ssh.v2.server_host_key.key_algorithm	ecdsa-sha2-nistp256
22.ssh.v2.support.client_to_server.ciphers	aes128-ctr, aes192-ctr, aes256-ctr…..
22.ssh.v2.support.client_to_server.compressions	none, zlib@openssh.com
22.ssh.v2.support.client_to_server.macs	hmac-md5-etm@openssh.com....
22.ssh.v2.support.first_kex_follows	False
22.ssh.v2.support.host_key_algorithms	ssh-rsa, ssh-dss….
22.ssh.v2.support.kex_algorithms	curve25519-sha256@libssh.org...
22.ssh.v2.support.server_to_client.ciphers	aes128-ctr, aes192-ctr, aes256-ctr…
22.ssh.v2.support.server_to_client.compressions	none, zlib@openssh.com
22.ssh.v2.support.server_to_client.macs	hmac-md5-etm@openssh.com

3.11 Survey of SSH server metadata

Let's explore SSH scanned. Using the search string

protocols.raw: "22/ssh"

then click **Metadata**, then click in the **Network Breakdown OVH, FR** or the web search string

(protocols.raw: "22/ssh") AND autonomous_system.description: "OVH, FR"

OVH doesn't have the best reputation in terms of proactive security on its network.

((protocols.raw: "22/ssh") AND autonomous_system.description: "OVH, FR") & 80.http.get.title: hacked

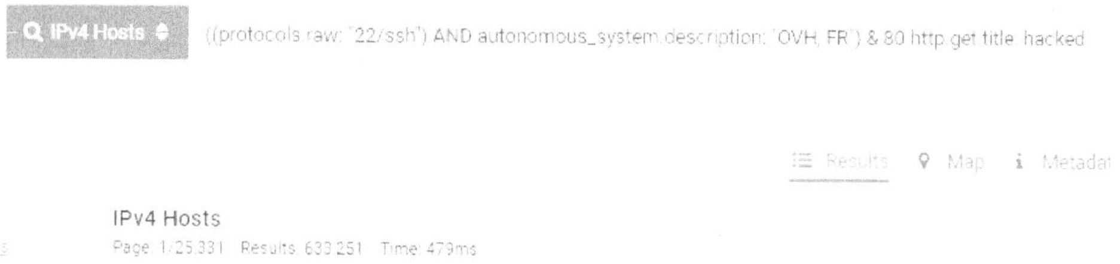

Figure 10 Censys OVH systems possibly hacked

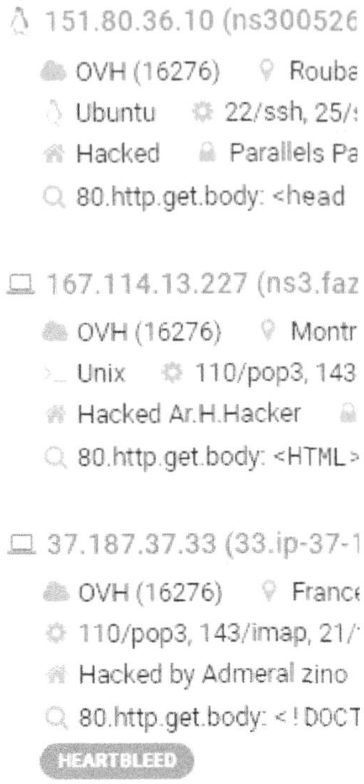

Figure 11 Censys 1st three OVH FR Hacked results

3.12 Exploring Telnet services

A top-rated podcast about hackers, major security incidents, viruses, worms and nation-state spy hacking called Darknet Diaries by Jack Rhysider. In episode 13 features a story about the Carna Botnet. In 2012, the botnet didn't destroy systems or disrupt the internet. Instead, it created a map of the internet by scanning all internet facing systems that responded. The scan highlighted the public, weak protocol Telnet's use across the internet. Telnet is still quite prevalent across the internet, as you'll soon find out. All Telnet credentials are sent in the clear, no encryption. It's highly recommended to switch from Telnet to SSH.

Telnet can also use port 2323, and Censys scans this port as Telnet. Any Telnet searches and fields can use the alternate port 2323 instead of port 23..

Table 20 Important Censys Telnet field examples

Censys field	Example
23.telnet.banner.banner	Please Log in Username:
23.telnet.banner.do	{u'name': u'Echo', u'value': 1}, {u'name': u'Suppress Go Ahead', u'value': 3}
23.telnet.banner.support	True
23.telnet.banner.metadata.version	
23.telnet.banner.will.name	Encryption Option

Table 21 Telnet fields

Censys field	Type
23.telnet.banner.banner	Text
23.telnet.banner.do.name	Keyword string
23.telnet.banner.do.value	Long unsigned 32 bit Integer
23.telnet.banner.dont.name	Keyword string
23.telnet.banner.dont.value	Long unsigned 32 bit Integer

23.telnet.banner.metadata.decription	Text
23.telnet.banner.metadata.manufacturer	Text
23.telnet.banner.metadata.product	Text
23.telnet.banner.metadata.revision	Text
23.telnet.banner.metadata.version	Text
23.telnet.banner.support	Boolean
23.telnet.banner.timestamp	Date time stamp
23.telnet.banner.will.name	Keyword string
23.telnet.banner.will.value	Long unsigned 32 bit Integer
23.telnet.banner.wont.name	Keyword string
23.telnet.banner.wont.value	Long unsigned 32 bit Integer

3.13 Discovering vulnerable Telnet service banners and settings

It's difficult to quantify what is considered weak or vulnerable Telnet because the protocol itself is considered insecure and its usage not recommended. The web search, using IPv4 will use the protocol, a NOT statement and known Telnet Will Banner Name text. Looking for Telnet without encryption options listed in the will name field.

(protocols.raw: "23/telnet") NOT 23.telnet.banner.will.name: "Encryption Option"

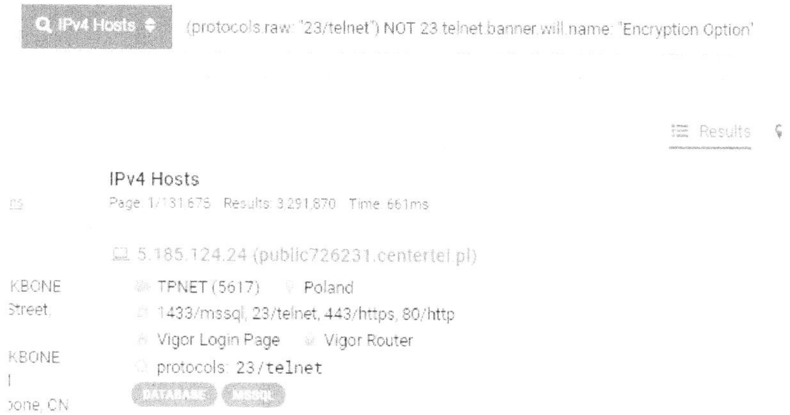

Figure 12 Censys search of Telnet excluding encryption options

CASE STUDY: Trump Towers Toronto

After a long 12 hour day teaching a GPEN course. I received a message from a friend in Eastern Europe on the 28th of September, 2016 about the Clinton-Trump presidential debate. Tired, blurry eyed, not able to watch the debate, the message "400lb hacker" was not immediately understood. Thinking damn, I'm not that chunky dude! My friend clarified and explained Trump's comments regarding hackers. Offended even more, by Trump, I messaged my friend back "give me a few minutes". Finding a gem in four minutes flat.

The State of New York weeks earlier fined Trump Towers $50,000 for poor digital security practices. It took about four minutes using a simple keyword search: **Trump + Hotel** to discover an FTP server. Trump Towers International Toronto used an old, outdated, insecure FTP for remote and financial management called Filezilla 0.9.39 beta. The same version I taught students in my GPEN course to exploit.

Smiling, I messaged my friend back with the find. To be nice, also tried to message the hotel and Trump to no avail. Many months later, I double checked if the same FileZilla FTP server and version was still exposed on the internet. Using Telnet with a CMD prompt or Terminal banner grabs the FTP version. So sad!

ftp 24.114.221.116

```
C:\Users\[redacted]>ftp 24.114.221.116
Connected to 24.114.221.116.
220-FileZilla Server version 0.9.39 beta
220 TRUMP International Hotel and Tower Toronto (FTP site)
530 Please log in with USER and PASS first.
User (24.114.221.116:(none)):
```

Figure 13 Trump Towers Toronto FileZilla beta version 3/2018

References

Darknet Diaries Episode 13 Carna Botnet
https://darknetdiaries.com/episode/13/

Ylonen, Tatu. "History of the SSH Protocol". *SSH home page. SSH Communications Security, Inc.* Retrieved 14 June 2017.

Chapter 4

SMTP/S, IMAP/S & POP3/S

INFORMATION IN THIS CHAPTER:

- Email protocols
- Email encryption opportunistic
- Email encryption misconfigurations
- Where to check DMARC and other email protocol settings beyond Censys

Opportunity is a haughty goddess who wastes no time with those who are unprepared.

- George S. Clason

4 Email

4.1 Introduction to Censys Email Protocols

Email servers and related protocols make up over 11% of the hosts scanned by Censys. Sending and receiving emails can enable businesses, people, or cripple communications if there is a major outage. In 2000, it was estimated the ILOVEYOU (Wikipedia 2018) virus, a mass email worm caused US$5.5-8.7 billion in damages. The virus caused network congestion, overloaded email servers, overwrote files and caused general mayhem. Outdated email servers might be vulnerable to DoS, remote control, manipulation of messages, eavesdropping, spamming; or if misconfigured, used as a malicious mail relay or used in fraud and phishing attacks.

Table 22 Censys 15/11/17 Host Report POP3/S & IMAP/S

Protocol	Number	Percentage
SMTP	7,363,711	3.23%
POP3	5,224,945	2.29%
IMAP	4,643,772	2.04%
IMAPS	4,381,536	1.92%
POP3S	4,056,349	1.78%
Total	25,670,313	11.26%

4.2 Exploring SMTP

Simple Mail Transport Protocol (SMTP) is the primary email transport protocol utilised, with a default port 25. By default the protocol is insecure; however, it can be secured by using valid certificates or enabling strict or opportunistic TLS encryption. Certificates can be self-signed, expired, weak ciphers, or misconfigured, nullifying any security benefit. The SMTP protocol can disclose information unintentionally, or implemented poorly. Lots of things can go wrong with SMTP security which attackers can take advantage.

Censys.io has over 200 SMTP related reportable fields. We'll focus on a few important ones which tend to yield good results.

Table 23 Important Censys SMTP fields & examples

SMTP field	Description
25.smtp	General port 25 SMTP search
25.smtp.starttls	The Start TLS code
25.smtp.starttls.ehlo	The general settings of the SMTP server
25.smtp.starttls.starttls.raw	
25.smtp.starttls.banner	

Table 24 SMTP Protocol Codes

SMTP Code	Description
211	System status / system help reply
214	Help message
220	Domain service ready
221	Domain service closing transmission channel
250	Requested mail action completed and OK
251	Not Local User, forward email to forward path
252	Cannot Verify user, will attempt delivery later
253	Pending messages for node started
354	Start mail input; end with

355	Octet-offset is the transaction offset
421	Domain service not available, closing transmission channel
432	Domain service not available, closing transmission channel
450	Requested mail action not taken: mailbox unavailable. request refused
451	Requested action aborted: local error in processing Request is unable to be processed, try again
452	Requested action not taken: insufficient system storage
453	No mail
454	TLS not available due to temporary reason. Encryption required for requested authentication mechanism
458	Unable to queue messages for node
459	Node not allowed: reason
500	Syntax error, command unrecognized
501	Syntax error in parameters or arguments
502	Command not implemented
503	Bad sequence of commands
504	Command parameter not implemented
510	Check the recipient address
512	Domain can not be found. Unknown host.

515	Destination mailbox address invalid
517	Problem with senders mail attribute, check properties
521	Domain does not accept mail
522	Recipient has exceeded mailbox limit
523	Server limit exceeded. Message too large
530	Access Denied. Authentication required
531	Mail system Full
533	Remote server has insufficient disk space to hold email
534	Authentication mechanism is too weak. Message too big
535	Multiple servers using same IP. Required Authentication
538	Encryption required for requested authentication mechanism
540	Email address has no DNS Server
541	No response from host
542	Bad Connection
543	Routing server failure. No available route
546	Email looping
547	Delivery time-out
550	Requested action not taken: mailbox unavailable

551	User not local; please try forward path
552	Requested mail action aborted: exceeded storage allocation
553	Requested action not taken: mailbox name not allowed
554	Transaction failed

The X can be 2, 4 or 5. 2 is success, 4 temporary problem and 5 permanent or fatal error occurred. 4.4.3 is a temporary error with a routing server failure.

http://www.inmotionhosting.com/support/email/email-troubleshooting/smtp-and-esmtp-error-code-list

Table 25 SMTP Extended codes ESMTP

SMTP Extended Code	Description
X.1.0	Other address status
X.1.1	Bad destination mailbox address
X.1.2	Bad destination system address
X.1.3	Bad destination mailbox address syntax
X.1.4	Destination mailbox address ambiguous
X.1.5	Destination mailbox address valid
X.1.6	Mailbox has moved
X.1.7	Bad sender's mailbox address syntax
X.1.8	Bad sender's system address

X.2.0	Other or undefined mailbox status
X.2.1	Mailbox disabled, not accepting messages
X.2.2	Mailbox full
X.2.3	Message length exceeds administrative limit
X.2.4	Mailing list expansion issue
X.3.0	Other or undefined mail system status
X.3.1	Mail system full
X.3.2	System not accepting network messages
X.3.3	System not capable of selected features
X.3.4	Message too big for system
X.3.5	System incorrectly configured
X.4.0	Other or undefined network or routing status
X.4.1	No answer from host
X.4.2	Bad connection
X.4.3	Routing server failure
X.4.4	Unable to route
X.4.5	Network congestion or insufficient disk
X.4.6	Routing loop detected
X.4.7	Delivery time expired
X.5.0	Other or undefined protocol status
X.5.1	Invalid command

X.5.2	Syntax error
X.5.3	Too many recipients
X.5.4	Invalid command arguments
X.5.5	Wrong protocol version
X.6.0	Other or undefined media error
X.6.1	Media not supported
X.6.2	Conversion required and prohibited
X.6.3	Conversion required but not supported
X.6.4	Conversion with loss performed
X.6.5	Conversion failed
X.7.0	Other or undefined security status
X.7.1	Delivery not authorized, message refused
X.7.2	Mailing list expansion prohibited
X.7.3	Security conversion required but not possible
X.7.4	Security features not supported
X.7.5	Cryptographic failure
X.7.6	Cryptographic algorithm not supported
X.7.7	Message integrity failure

Example 1 25.smtp.starttls example output

Reporting field	Example output

25.smtp.starttls	220 Begin TLS negotiation

Example 2 25.smtp.starttls.ehlo example output

Reporting field	Example output
25.smtp.starttls.ehlo	250-cloudserver1234.home.net.com Hello CLIENT_HOSTNAME X.4.1[CLIENT_IP], pleased to meet you X.4.2 250-PIPELINING 250-ENHANCEDSTATUSCODES 250-SIZE 250-8BITMIME 250-STARTTLS 250-AUTH PLAIN LOGIN 250-AUTH=PLAIN LOGIN 250 HELP

4.3 Discovering SMTP Metadata

In the web search, IPv4, use the search string then select **Metadata**

protocols.raw: "25/smtp"

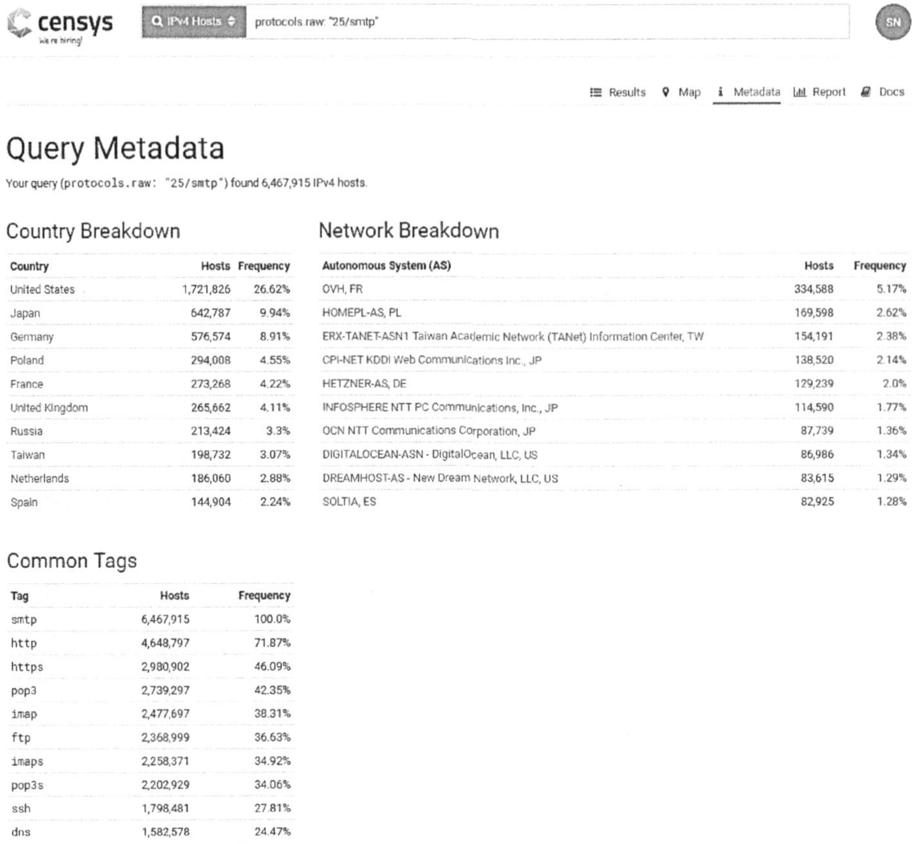

censys
We're hiring!
IPv4 Hosts | protocols.raw: "25/smtp"

Results | Map | Metadata | Report | Docs

Query Metadata

Your query (`protocols.raw: "25/smtp"`) found 6,467,915 IPv4 hosts.

Country Breakdown

Country	Hosts	Frequency
United States	1,721,826	26.62%
Japan	642,787	9.94%
Germany	576,574	8.91%
Poland	294,008	4.55%
France	273,268	4.22%
United Kingdom	265,662	4.11%
Russia	213,424	3.3%
Taiwan	198,732	3.07%
Netherlands	186,060	2.88%
Spain	144,904	2.24%

Network Breakdown

Autonomous System (AS)	Hosts	Frequency
OVH, FR	334,588	5.17%
HOMEPL-AS, PL	169,598	2.62%
ERX-TANET-ASN1 Taiwan Academic Network (TANet) Information Center, TW	154,191	2.38%
CPI-NET KDDI Web Communications Inc., JP	138,520	2.14%
HETZNER-AS, DE	129,239	2.0%
INFOSPHERE NTT PC Communications, Inc., JP	114,590	1.77%
OCN NTT Communications Corporation, JP	87,739	1.36%
DIGITALOCEAN-ASN - DigitalOcean, LLC, US	86,986	1.34%
DREAMHOST-AS - New Dream Network, LLC, US	83,615	1.29%
SOLTIA, ES	82,925	1.28%

Common Tags

Tag	Hosts	Frequency
smtp	6,467,915	100.0%
http	4,648,797	71.87%
https	2,980,902	46.09%
pop3	2,739,297	42.35%
imap	2,477,697	38.31%
ftp	2,368,999	36.63%
imaps	2,258,371	34.92%
pop3s	2,202,929	34.06%
ssh	1,798,481	27.81%
dns	1,582,578	24.47%

Figure 14 Censys SMTP protocol Metadata

Table 26 Censys SMTP Metadata Country Breakdown

Country	Hosts	Frequency
United States	1,721,826	26.62%
Japan	642,787	9.94%
Germany	576,574	8.91%
Poland	294,008	4.55%
France	273,268	4.22%
United Kingdom	265,662	4.11%

Russia	213,424	3.3%
Taiwan	198,732	3.07%
Netherlands	186,060	2.88%
Spain	144,904	2.24%

Table 27 Censys SMTP Metadata Network Breakdown

Autonomous Systems (AS)	Hosts	Frequency
OVH, FR	334,588	5.17%
HOMEPL-AS, PL	169,598	2.62%
ERX-TANET-ASN1 Taiwan Academic Network (TANet) Information Center, TW	154,191	2.38%
CPI-NET KDDI Web Communications Inc., JP	138,520	2.14%
HETZNER-AS, DE	129,239	2.0%
INFOSPHERE NTT PC Communications, Inc., JP	114,590	1.77%
OCN NTT Communications Corporation, JP	87,739	1.36%
DIGITALOCEAN-ASN - DigitalOcean, LLC, US	86,986	1.34%
DREAMHOST-AS - New Dream Network, LLC, US	83,615	1.29%
SOLTIA, ES	82,925	1.28%

Table 28 Censys SMTP Metadata Common Tags

Tag	Hosts	Frequency
smtp	6,467,915	100.0%
http	4,648,797	71.87%
https	2,980,902	46.09%
pop3	2,739,297	42.35%
imap	2,477,697	38.31%
ftp	2,368,999	36.63%
imaps	2,258,371	34.92%
pop3s	2,202,929	34.06%
ssh	1,798,481	27.81%
dns	1,582,578	24.47%

4.4 Discovering SMTP Start TLS configuration

Email protocols, as initially written, had no forethought of security. As such, a pen tester can leverage the default settings of various email protocols to their advantage. Censys returns various SMTP fields and configurations. However, it's always better to use a scientific method and cross-check the properties with additional tools.

4.4.1 SSL-Tools.net

A secondary web based tool can be used to check TLS status to compare against Censys detailed results if you have access and can send from the domain. Send an empty email, no subject line or body to: check@ssl-tools.net

Figure 15 SSL-Tools.net Start TLS Configuration Tester

4.4.2 Netcraft.com

If you don't have access to the email server, fear not for a secondary tool to cross check. Use Netcraft.com, which scans higher popularity internet-connected systems, reporting web and email banners. Go to Netcraft.com then What's that site running? Fill in a domain name, then press the arrow to search.

Figure 16 Netcraft.com What's that site running? domain tool

Then press the report icon under Site Report, this URL will also function:

https://toolbar.netcraft.com/site_report?url=http://www.dod.gov

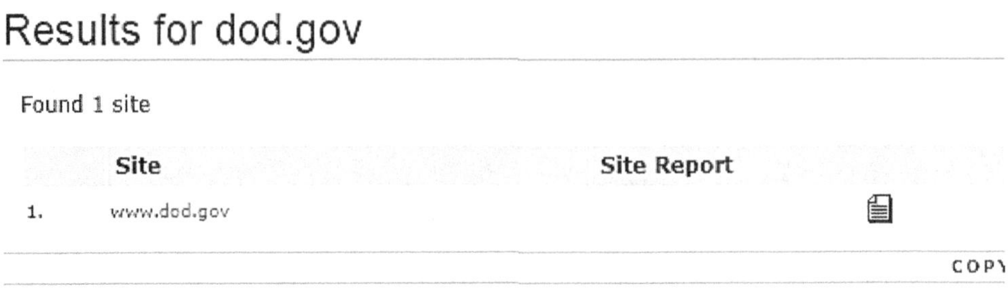

Figure 17 Netcraft.com Results for DOD.gov

Look at the properties for Sender Policy Framework and DMARC.

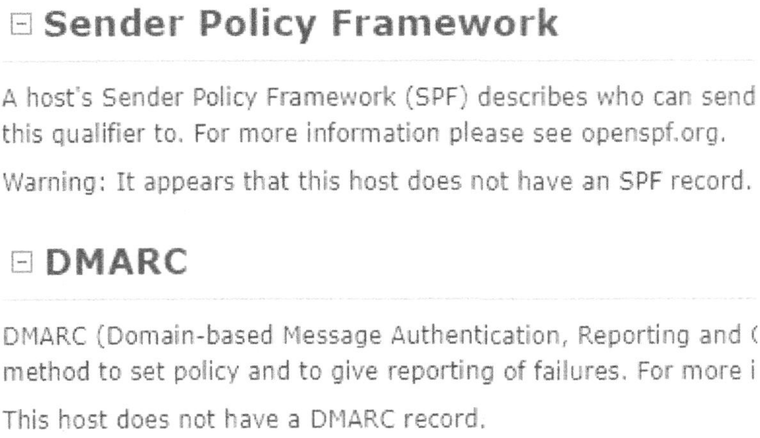

Figure 18 Summary of DOD.gov SPF & DMARC settings via Netcraft.com

4.5 Systems with TLS failures caused by misconfigurations

There are two SMTP properties we are looking at, TLS failure to start and a system misconfigured. Using the tables for SMTP codes and SMTP Extended codes ESMTP. Both conditions and fields need to match. The TLS Start field is **25.smtp.starttls.starttls**. The **X** in the ESMTP can be variable, but 4 is temporary, which describes most misconfigurations.

SMTP Code/Extended	Description
454	TLS not available due to temporary reason. Encryption required for requested authentication mechanism
X.3.5	System incorrectly configured

This translates into the search query: **(25.smtp.starttls.starttls) AND 25.smtp.starttls.starttls: "4.3.5"**

If you are logged in, the direct URL on Censys is: **https://censys.io/ipv4?q=%2825.smtp.starttls.starttls%29+AND+25.smtp.starttls.starttls%3A+"4.3.5"**

Figure 19 Censys SMTP Unable to start code

There are several ways to find these types of misconfigured hosts. Keyword searches, dorking SMTP banners can also be utilized.

4.6 TLS not available email systems

There are two SMTP properties we are looking at, TLS not available and a general information variable why this feature cannot be used by the email server. Using the tables for SMTP codes and SMTP Extended codes ESMTP. Both conditions and fields need to match. The TLS Start field is **25.smtp.starttls.starttls**. The **X** in the ESMTP can be variable but 4 is temporary, which describes most misconfigurations.

SMTP Code/Extended	Description

454	TLS not available due to temporary reason. Encryption required for requested authentication mechanism
X.1.0	Other address status (Variable)

This translates into the search query: **(25.smtp.starttls.starttls) AND 25.smtp.starttls.starttls: "4.1.0"**

Figure 20 Censys SMTP TLS not available code

4.7 Email servers with insufficient disk space or network congestion

Helpful if double checking if a DoS/DDoS attack is working against an email server, a bottle neck or network problems.

SMTP Code/Extended	Description
454	TLS not available due to temporary reason. Encryption required for requested authentication mechanism
X.4.5	Network congestion or insufficient disk

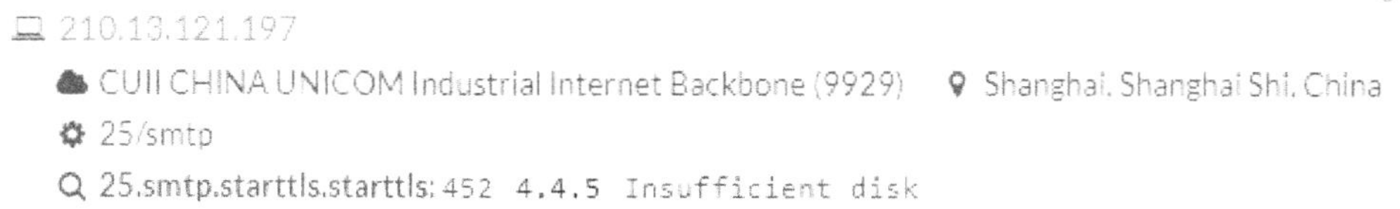

Figure 21 Censys SMTP Insufficient disk space

4.8 Censys search results for range of SMTP extended codes

Searching using ranges can include IP addresses, protocol codes, software versions, etc. Search using the IPv4 option, the range of SMTP codes.

(25.smtp.starttls) AND 25.smtp.starttls.starttls: [4.1.0 to 4.3.5]

Figure 22 Censys web search using a range of SMTP extended codes

CASE STUDY: Strip Start-TLS and EU GDPR

Privacy stripped away, one email at a time

As the European Union General Data Protection Regulations (EU GDPR) came into force, a privacy stripping email setting continues in widespread use around the world. It threatens sensitive communications that contains personally-identifiable information, intellectual property, financial information, and your most intimate photos.

You might log in to an email account to use it, but that doesn't mean your messages are sent securely. Contrary to the assumption of privacy, a username and password may provide, by default, emails are sent unencrypted unless explicitly or opportunistically secured. Email technology standards were written in a more innocent time before severe concerns about confidentiality.

Email privacy became a significant concern to the EU public after the Prism disclosures. Suddenly, the non-technical IT world began to understand how damaging lack of email encryption could be. After the Snowden revelations, providers like Gmail, Hotmail, private companies and many others decided to try and secure email communications.

Configuring explicit security is not easy. It requires overhead and certificate management. Opportunistic security can help fill the gap. Encrypt email wherever possible, opportunistically, with a setting called Start-TLS. This opportunistically scrambles email contents to prevent eavesdropping. The setting, called Start-TLS, can provide a basic level or retain privacy protection. It's not a guarantee, but helpful, similar to the HTTPS Encrypt Everywhere movement.

On the flip side, is a configuration which does the opposite, Strip-Start TLS. This email server setting removes any opportunistic encryption on emails, stripping them, baring the contents of the conversation.

Why is this important?

CASE STUDY: Strip Start-TLS and EU GDPR

Back in 2014, the EFF reviewed an engineer's blog post from Golden Frog VPN describing the problem. The engineer could no longer send and receive encrypted emails to a customer because an ISP provider applied the Strip Start-TLS setting. Leaving communications bare to eavesdropping. Anyone, hacking tool, criminal, spy agency could potentially read the emails.

From Wikipedia " Opportunistic TLS is an opportunistic encryption mechanism. Because the initial handshake takes place in plain text, an attacker in control of the network can modify the server messages via a man-in-the-middle attack to make it appear that TLS is unavailable (called a STRIPTLS attack). Most SMTP clients will then send the email and possibly passwords in plain text, often with no notification to the user. In particular, many SMTP connections occur between mail servers, where user notification is not practical."

If anyone doubts how valuable email communications are, or if such all you can eat buffet programs like Prism exist. While crafting an OSINT hacking crash course for Security BSides LV 2017, four NSA Prism related subdomains popped up using a web-based reconnaissance tool.

portal.nsa.gov, pretenders.nsa.gov, prism.nsa.gov, prism1.nsa.gov, prism2.nsa.gov,
prism3.nsa.gov, remoteoffice.nsa.gov, remoteoffice1.nsa.gov, remoteoffice2.nsa.gov,

Figure 23 Highlighted list of NSA subdomains listing Prism July 2017

Have things changed much in the last few years? Sadly, a resounding no. Even with existing data protection laws across Europe, the USA, other concerned countries, the Strip Start TLS configuration is in widespread use. Some vendors like Cisco, have Strip Start TLS seemingly ingrained in their product lines.

Use of the setting without notification could be contrary to the EU-US data privacy shield. Multiple USA based EU partners under new EU-US Privacy Shield agreements use strip opportunistic email encryption.

CASE STUDY: Strip Start-TLS and EU GDPR

The disturbing email anti-privacy setting can be easily found. Using Censys.io tags, and two Python-based tools: ZMAP and StripTLS.

Using Censys.io, a simple search yielded 11,641 in a few seconds, displaying many ISPs and email providers using the Strip Start-TLS tag. The tag is applied to a device based on metadata, technology in use and communications behaviour.

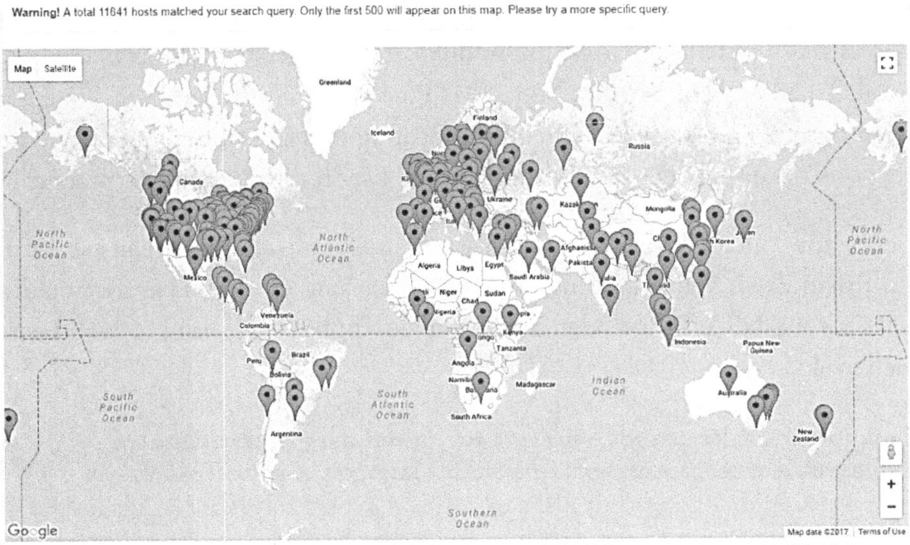

Figure 24 Censys.io Strip Start-TLS global scan 10 November 2017

The USA returns the highest percentage of stripping systems on the internet—over six times the amount of China.

There is a confusing patchwork of data privacy laws at the federal and state level in the USA. However, the federal Health Insurance Portability and Accountability Act (HIPAA) broadly covers medial data privacy via a privacy and security rule.

Second on the list is the UK, with other European countries close by its side.

Country Breakdown

Country	Hosts	Frequency
United States	3,897	33.48%
United Kingdom	830	7.13%
China	627	5.39%
Russia	430	3.69%
France	401	3.44%
Australia	335	2.88%
Italy	295	2.53%
Canada	276	2.37%
Japan	222	1.91%
Germany	218	1.87%

Figure 25 Censys.io Strip Start-TLS top country report 10 November 2017

Focusing on the European content, over three-thousand email stripping servers are found, resulting in too many data points to fit on the map. Removing Russia from the list, and looking at EU GDPR locations only, the top five are: the UK, France, Italy, Germany and the Netherlands. Some of these areas have existing data protection laws, which cover email and legislate against the widespread collection of data and communications.

Figure 26 Censys.io Strip Start-TLS European scan 10 November 2017

CASE STUDY: Strip Start-TLS and EU GDPR

Country Breakdown

Country	Hosts	Frequency
United Kingdom	830	22.0%
Russia	440	11.66%
France	402	10.66%
Italy	306	8.11%
Germany	222	5.89%
Netherlands	174	4.61%
Romania	152	4.03%
Czech Republic	111	2.94%
Poland	107	2.84%
Spain	86	2.28%

Figure 27 Censys.io Strip Start-TLS top European country report 10 November 2017

The UK implemented their version of data privacy regulations, complete with major fining power. Violators risk possible financial penalties. Hidden behind the UK ISPs and data centre providers are banks, financial institutions like Rabobank and Santander, travel agency. Government councils, hosting, and other internet service providers like 1stdomains.co.uk and 1stdnsltd.co.uk.

Network Breakdown

Autonomous System (AS)	Hosts	Frequency
RACKSPACE-LON, GB	129	15.54%
BT-UK-AS BTnet UK Regional network, GB	72	8.67%
UKFAST, GB	66	7.95%
COGENT-174 - Cogent Communications, US	65	7.83%
NTL, GB	36	4.34%
IOMART-AS, GB	29	3.49%
NODE4-AS, GB	24	2.89%
COLT, GB	14	1.69%
CW Vodafone Group PLC, GB	13	1.57%
TELECITY-LON, GB	13	1.57%

Figure 28 Censys.io Strip Start-TLS top UK network providers report 10 November 2017

CASE STUDY: Strip Start-TLS and EU GDPR

BT on the other hand, appears to own and host several stripping systems, like the Thailand government. Most of the ISPs in the list own and host email security stripping systems. Many ISPs in France, Germany and Italy own email stripping systems.

Figure 29 Censys.io Strip Start TLS UK BT owned systems 15 November 2017

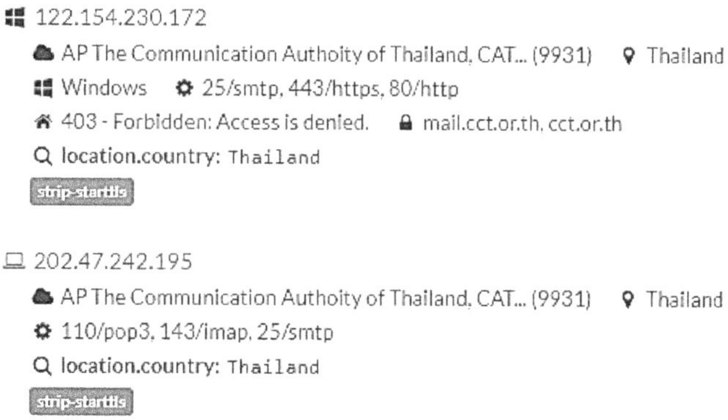

Figure 30 Censys.io Strip Start-TLS Thailand government telecommunications systems 15 November 2017

CASE STUDY: Strip Start-TLS and EU GDPR

Currently, I use the Netherlands as a base of operations. Zooming on the Dutch findings, 174 systems, some operated by ISPs, web hosting providers and private organizations around the country.

Network Breakdown

Autonomous System (AS)	Hosts	Frequency
LEASEWEB-NL Netherlands, NL	20	11.49%
ZIGGO Ziggo B.V., NL	15	8.62%
KPN This macro reflects our filtering-policy on, NL	14	8.05%
DDF-AS, NL	13	7.47%
XS4ALL-NL Amsterdam, NL	7	4.02%
COLOCENTER, NL	6	3.45%
KPN-INTERNEDSERVICES, NL	6	3.45%
LGI-UPC formerly known as UPC Broadband Holding B.V., AT	6	3.45%
ASN-ROUTIT, NL	5	2.87%
I3DNET, NL	5	2.87%

Figure 31 Censys.io Strip Start-TLS top NL network providers report 10 November 2017

194.151.115.165 (static.kpn.net)
KPN This macro reflects our filtering-policy on (1136) Netherlands
25/smtp
location.country: Netherlands
strip-starttls

217.166.217.99 (static.kpn.net)
KPN This macro reflects our filtering-policy on (1136) Netherlands
25/smtp
location.country: Netherlands
strip-starttls

Figure 32 Censys.io Strip Start TLS NL KPN Static owned systems 15 November 2017

CASE STUDY: Strip Start-TLS and EU GDPR

Similar to Thailand and other top EU countries on the tag list, most of the ISPs appear to own and host autonomous systems which strip opportunistic email encryption. KPN has several assets combined with a peering policy which stipulates data peers with KPN must also peer traffic to the USA wherever possible.

One of the pillars of the EU GDPR is consent and awareness of what is occurring with data. Encryption appears to be going backwards, not forwards. The surprising amount of these privacy stripping email systems on European networks, ISPs, web hosting, private organizations and internet network transits is disturbing to the privacy-conscious.

Most people are unaware email security can be downgraded, or previously secured emails exposed. Until EU data regulators gain awareness and clamp down on the illegitimate usage of Strip Start-TLS. The EU GDPR is impossible to implement if downgrading privacy and security across the EU is actively defeated broadly across the European internet.

Tools used for this case study

- Censys.io
- StripTLS python tool by tintinweb
- ZMAP.io
- The Internet

References

PRISM (surveillance program)
https://en.wikipedia.org/wiki/PRISM_(surveillance_program)

Chapter 5

Web technologies

INFORMATION IN THIS CHAPTER:

- Deeps dives into HTTP and HTTPS
- Codes & status of the protocols
- HTTP/S Metadata
- Insecure HTTPS certificate security discovery
- Case Study: Responsible disclosure to the NSA

He who would search for pearls must dive below.

- John Dryden

5 HTTP & HTTPS

5.1 Introduction to Censys HTTP/S Protocols

The majority of the internet systems which Censys scans using ZMAP utilise the HTTP and HTTPS protocols. Web pages for various purposes. Each week a general scan and host report are available, breaking down the composition of the hosts scanned. A November 2017 host report shows just over 50% of the hosts scanned are running HTTP or HTTPS services.

Table 29 Censys 15/11/17 Host Report HTTP and HTTPS

Protocol	Number	Percentage
HTTP	73,414,364	32.18%
HTTPS	41,548,182	18.21%
Total	114,962,546	50.39%

5.2 Exploring HTTP

The HyperText Transport Protocol (HTTP) is the protocol which provides primary, modern web pages and services. The default port is TCP 80; however, it can be found or run from any port. Ports 80, 8080, 8888 and 7547. Censys intends to add additional ports scanned for HTTP services in the future.

Valuable information can be found looking at the HTTP fields. Essential fields a security researcher will find useful.

- Header information displaying technology
- Metadata description displaying the technology and version
- Manufacturer and Vendor
- Metadata product name
- Metadata software version
- The status code
- Status line
- Header server version
- HTML body
- HTML Title
- Unknown headers can yield a diverse type of information
- Cross site scripting configuration settings
- Real IP address

Table 30 Important HTTP Censys fields & examples

Censys field	Example
80.http.get.headers	x_powered_by ASP.NET
80.http.get.metadata.description	Microsoft IIS 7.5
80.http.get.metadata.manufacturer	Microsoft
80.http.get.metadata.product	IIS
80.http.get.metadata.version	7.5
80.http.get.status_code	200
80.http.get.status_line	200 OK
80.http.get.headers.server	Microsoft-IIS/7.5
80.http.get.body	<html><head><title>Suspended Domain…..
80.http.get.title	Suspended Domain
80.http.get.headers.unknown	{u'value': u'Wed, 20 Dec 2017 20:15:29 GMT', u'key': u'date'}
80.http.get.headers.x_xss_protection	1; mode=block
80.http.get.headers.x_real_ip	10.112.10.1
80.http.get.headers.strict_transport_security	max-age=63072000; includeSubdomains;

The HTTP information codes will return the various HTTP codes numerically and a description for use as a string.

Table 31 HTTP Information Codes

HTTP Codes	Description
100	Information – Continue
101	Switching Protocol
102	Processing
103	Early Hints

The HTTP success codes will return the various HTTP codes numerically and a description for use as a string. Codes 207 and 208 WebDAV can be risky, this service has a history of vulnerabilities and exploits.

Table 32 HTTP Success Codes

HTTP Codes	Description
200	Successful – OK
201	Created
202	Accepted
203	Non-authoritative information (HTTP/1.1)
204	No content
205	Reset content
206	Partial content
207	Multi-status (WebDAV)
208	Already reported (WebDAV)

226	IM Used

The HTTP redirection codes will return the various HTTP codes numerically and a description for use as a string. These are good for both availability and security purposes.

Table 33 HTTP Redirection Codes

HTTP Codes	Description
300	Multiple choices
301	Moved permanently
302	Found
303	See Other (HTTP/1.1)
304	Mot modified
305	Use proxy (HTTP/1.1)
306	Switch proxy
307	Temporary redirect (HTTP/1.1)
308	Permanent redirect

The HTTP client error codes will return the various HTTP codes numerically and a description for use as a string. These are useful for many researchers, especially for finding teapots.

Table 34 HTTP Client Error Codes

HTTP Codes	Description
400	Bad request

401	Unauthorized
402	Payment required
403	Forbidden
404	Not found
405	Method not allowed
406	Not acceptable
407	Proxy authentication required
408	Request timeout
409	Conflict
410	Gone
411	Length required
412	Precondition failed
413	Payload too large
414	URI too long
415	Unsupported media type
416	Range not satisfiable
417	Expectation failed
418	I am a teapot (code should be returned by teapots requested to brew coffee) RFC 2324 😊
421	Misdirected request
422	Unprocessable entity (WebDAV)

423	Locked (WebDAV)
424	Failed dependency
426	Upgrade required
428	Precondition required
429	Too many requests
431	Request header fields too large
451	Unavailable for legal reasons (or not ready for the EU GDPR after >2 yrs. of notice to plan)

The HTTP server error codes will return the various HTTP codes numerically and a description for use as a string. Most of these codes can be used for availability, security purposes and with code 511, can indicate interesting logging portal services and "legal" interception/ deep packet inspection/ sucks up all internet traffic devices like a hoover.

Table 35 HTTP Server Error Codes

HTTP Code	Description
500	Internal server error
501	Not implemented
502	Bad gateway
503	Service unavailable
504	Gateway timeout
505	HTTP version not supported

506	Variant also negotiates
507	Insufficient storage (WebDAV)
508	Loop detected
510	Not extended
511	Network authentication required (captive portals, intercepting proxies)

The HTTP unofficial codes will return the various HTTP codes numerically and a description for use as a string. Code 420 is beginning to get used much more often.

Table 36 HTTP Unofficial Codes

HTTP Code	Description
103	Checkpoint
420	Method Failure (Spring Framework)
420	Enhance Your Calm (Twitter API rate limited)
429	Too Many Requests (Twitter >1.1)
450	Blocked by Parental Controls (Microsoft)
498	Invalid or Expired Token (Esri)
509	Bandwidth Limit Exceeded (Apache Web Server/cPanel)
530	Site is frozen (Pantheon)
598	Network read timeout error (some HTTP Proxies)

The HTTP Microsoft Internet Information codes are specific to

Microsoft's ISS web server and will return the various HTTP codes numerically and a description for use as a string.

Table 37 Microsoft Internet Information Services HTTP Codes

HTTP Codes	Description
440	Login time-out
449	Retry with
451	Redirect

The HTTP NGINX codes are specific to NGINX's web server and will return the various HTTP codes numerically and a description for use as a string.

Table 38 NGINX HTTP Error Codes

HTTP Codes	Description
444	No response
495	SSL certificate error
496	SSL certificate required
497	HTTP request sent to HTTPS port
499	Client closed request

Censys IPv4 search string:

80.http.get.status_code: 495

80.http.get.metadata.product	nginx
80.http.get.metadata.version	1.12.2
80.http.get.status_code	495
80.http.get.status_line	495 status code 495
80.http.get.title	SSL certificate error

Figure 33 80.http.get.status_code: 495

Table 39 HTTP 500 error codes

HTTP Codes	Description
520	Unknown error
521	Web server us down
522	Connection timed out
523	Origin is unreachable
524	A timeout occurred
525	SLL handshake failed
526	Invalid SSL certificate
527	Railgun error

5.3 Find H?cked webpages

There are many ways to find hacked websites with Censys. This is a simple method which also shows how Censys uses characters like " ? " Further searches can be refined to focus on a higher percentage of actual hacked systems and websites.

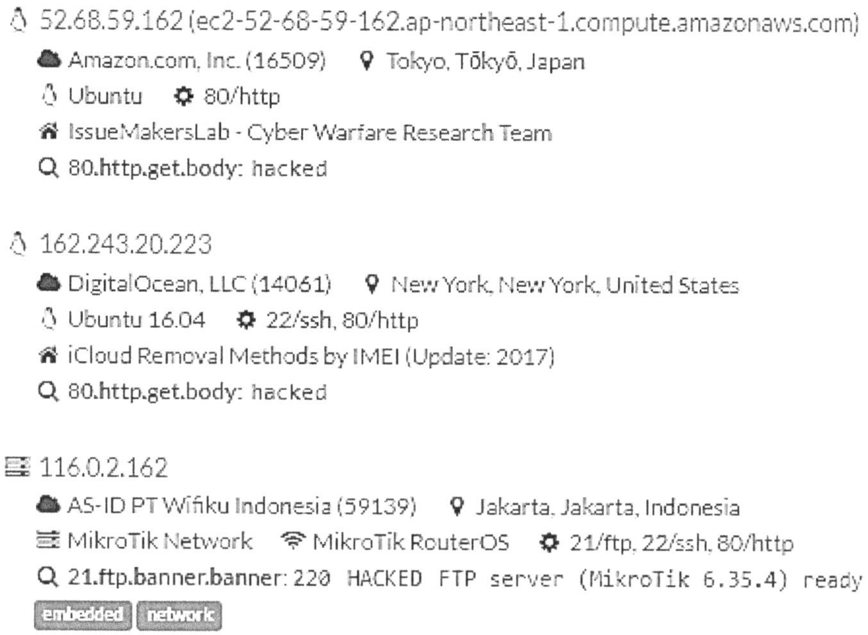

Figure 34 Censys web search "H?cked" using ? to replace a letter

5.4 Find Teapots

HTTP 418 is from an request for comments (RFC) on April Fools in 1998 (Wikipedia 2017). Yes, technologists have humour 😊

80.http.get.status_line: 418

Figure 35 Censys web search "HTTP 418 I'm a teapot"

5.4 Exploring HTTPS

The Secure Hyper Text Transport Protocol (HTTPS) is the protocol which provides basic, secure, modern web pages and services. The default port is TCP 443, however, like HTTP, it can be found or run from any port.

Table 40 Important HTTPS Censys fields & examples

Censys field	Example
443.https.tls.certificate.parsed.names	Autodiscover.cdc.gov, externalews.cdc.gov, Webmail.cdc.gov
443.https.tls.certificate.parsed.fingerprint_md5	368cfd1e232121868aed4e4e825b6348
443.https.tls.certificate.parsed.signature.self_signed	False
443.https.tls.certificate.parsed.signature_algorithm.name	SHA256WithRSA
443.https.tls.certificate.parsed.subject.common_name	cdcmail.cdc.gov
443.https.tls.certificate.parsed.subject.country	US
443.https.tls.certificate.parsed.subject.locality	Atlanta
443.https.tls.signature.hash_algorithm	sha256
443.https.tls.certificate.parsed.subject.organization	Centers for Disease Control and Prevention
443.https.tls.certificate.parsed.subje	CDCMail

ct.organizational_unit	
443.https.tls.signature.signature_algorithm	rsa
443.https.tls.signature.valid	True
443.https.tls.version	TLSv1.2
443.https.heartbleed.heartbleed_vulnerable	False
zlint.errors_present	False
zlint.fatals_present	False
zlint.lints.n_subject_common_name_included	True
zlint.version	3
zlint.warnings_present	False
443.https.tls.certificate.parsed.extensions.subject_alt_name.dns_names	m.nsa.gov

5.5 Finding IIS server usage in the Top Million websites

Right Click search
(80.http.get.headers.server: IIS) AND 80.http.get.headers.server: "IIS"
It looks at the top million websites

fnb.co.za
2,298 25/smtp, 443/https, 443/https_www, 80/http, 80/http_www
Home - First National Bank - FNB fnb.co.za, fnbnamibia.com.na, fnb.co.ls
80.http_www.get.headers.server: IIS

5.5 Find Heartbleed vulnerable systems in the Ukraine

This is a nifty, easy search to find Heartbleed systems using the IPv4 web search. It uses both the country code and a Boolean True value.

location.country_code: UA AND 443.https.heartbleed.heartbleed_vulnerable: true

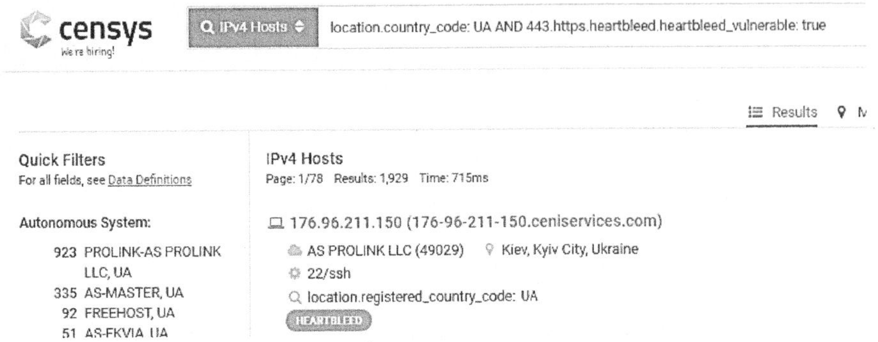

Figure 36 Censys Ukrainian Heartbleed vulnerable search result

5.6 HTTPS Tags

Detailed HTTP tags and fields for searches.

Table 41 Censys HTTPS HTTP certificate Tags

HTTPS Tags
Unexpired
Never Trusted
Leaf
CT
Google CT
DV

Currently Trusted
Expired
Self-Signed
Previously Trusted
EV
CT PreCert
Intermediate
CCADB
Redacted

Table 42 Censys HTTPS certificate fields

Certificate fields
ct.behind_the_sofa
ct.censys.
ct.censys_dev
ct.certificatetransparency_cn_ct
ct.certly_log
ct.cloudflare_nimbus_2017
ct.cloudflare_nimbus_2018
ct.cloudflare_nimbus_2019
ct.cloudflare_nimbus_2020

ct.cloudflare_nimbus_2021	
ct.cnnic_ctserver.sct	
ct.comodo_dodo	
ct.comodo_mammoth	
ct.comodo_sabre	
ct.digicert_ct1	
ct.digicert_ct2	
ct.gdca_ct	
ct.gdca_log	
ct.gdca_log2	
ct.google_argon2017	
ct.google_argon2018	
ct.google_argon2019	
ct.google_argon2020	
ct.google_argon2021	
ct.google_aviator	
ct.google_daedalus	
ct.google_icarus	
ct.google_pilot	
ct.google_rocketeer	
ct.google_skydiver	

ct.google_submariner
ct.google_testtube
ct.izenpe_com
ct.izenpe_eus
ct.letsencrypt_ct_clicky
ct.nordu_ct_plausable
ct.sheca_ct
ct.startssl_ct
ct.symantec_ws_ct
ct.symantec_ws_deneb
ct.symantec_ws_sirus
ct.symantec_ws_vega
ct.venafi_api_ctlog
ct.wosign_ct
ct.wosign_ctlog
ct.wotrus_ctlog

Table 43 Censys HTTPS Parsed certificate fields

Certificate fields
parsed.extensions
parsed.extensions.extended_key_usage.ipsec_end_system

parsed.extensions.extended_key_usage.ipsec_user
parsed.extensions
parsed.extensions
parsed.extensions

5.7 Finding Hacked Let's Encrypt certificates

Use a Censys IPv4 web based search string. Hacked Let's Encrypt certificates can be discovered. This is useful to check your organisation's certificates or a client's.

(Hacked) AND parsed.issuer.organization.raw: "Let's Encrypt"

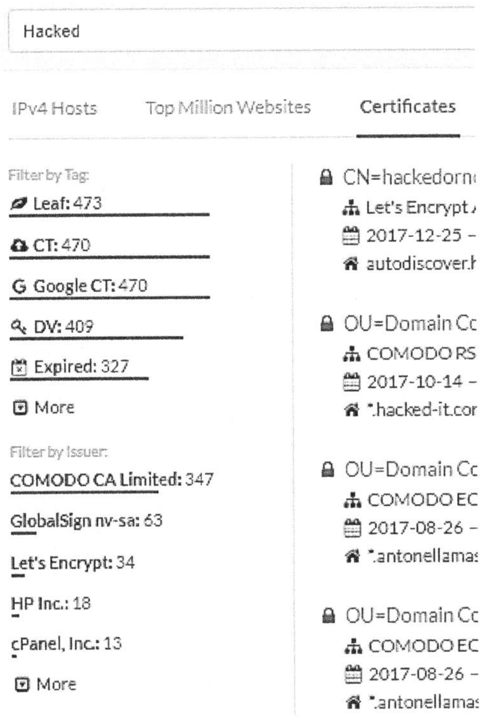

Figure 37 Censys Hacked certificate search

(Hacked) AND parsed.issuer.organization.raw: "Let's Encrypt"

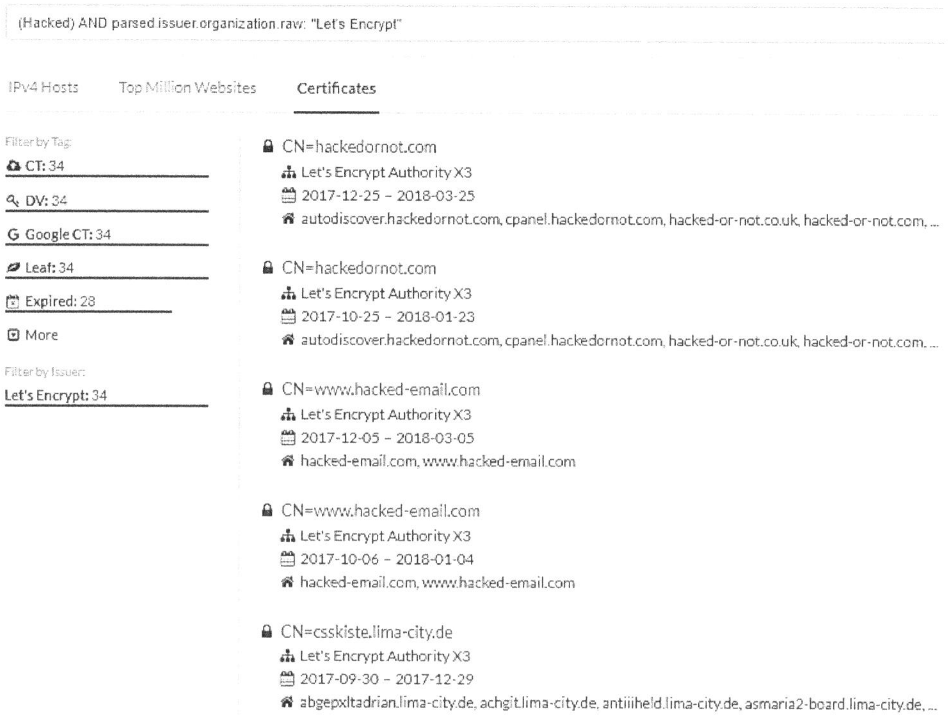

Figure 38 (Hacked) AND parsed.issuer.organization.raw: "Let's Encrypt"

5.8 Find HTTPS using a known private key

This is a fun search, because there are so many internet facing systems using known private keys.

protocols.raw: "443/https" and tags:known-private-key

Figure 39 Censys HTTPS & known private keys

5.9 Find weak encryption cipher protocols used by HTTP/S & SSH

This is a general search to find the weak protocols MD5, SHA0, SHA1, DES and RC4 used by internet exposed systems. OWASP's testing guide lists this search Testing for Weak Encryption OTG-CRYPST-004. OWASP lists the following encryption algorithms as weak:

- MD4
- MD5
- RC4
- RC2
- DES
- Blowfish
- SHA-1
- ECB

Search with IPv4 using the keyword search inside protocols, the query the **Metadata**.

protocols: md5, sha0, sha1, des, rc4

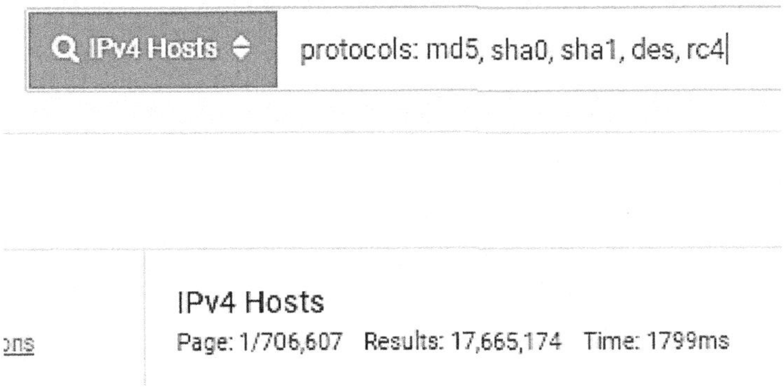

Figure 40 Censys weak encryption protocols search

Country Breakdown

Country	Hosts	Frequency
United States	7,302,397	41.32%
China	1,266,931	7.17%
Germany	1,010,036	5.72%
United Kingdom	667,533	3.78%
France	654,788	3.71%
Canada	591,188	3.35%
Russia	518,407	2.93%
Netherlands	425,125	2.41%
Brazil	368,809	2.09%
Italy	305,885	1.73%

Figure 41 Censys weak encryption protocols search Country Breakdown

Press the country of China or use the direct search string in IPv4.

(protocols: md5, sha0, sha1, des, rc4) AND location.country: "China"

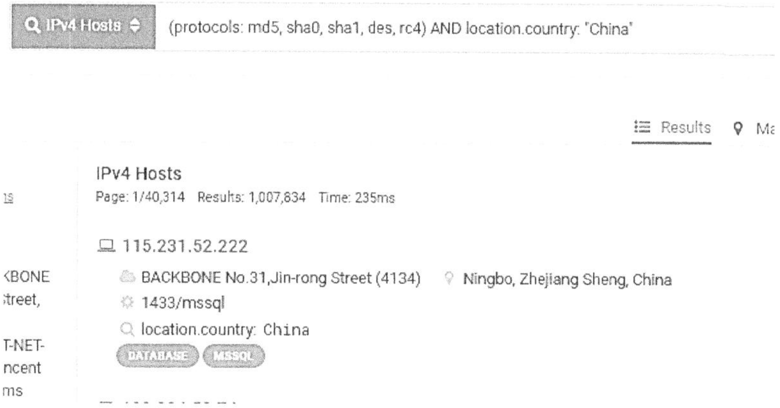

Figure 42 Censys search results weak Chinese encryption

5.11 Discovering expired NSA.gov certificates

Using the Censys Certificates web search option, you will search for any NSA.gov expired certificates. The web search is **Certificates** search, using the domain and Tag **Expired**.

(nsa.gov) AND tags.raw: "expired"

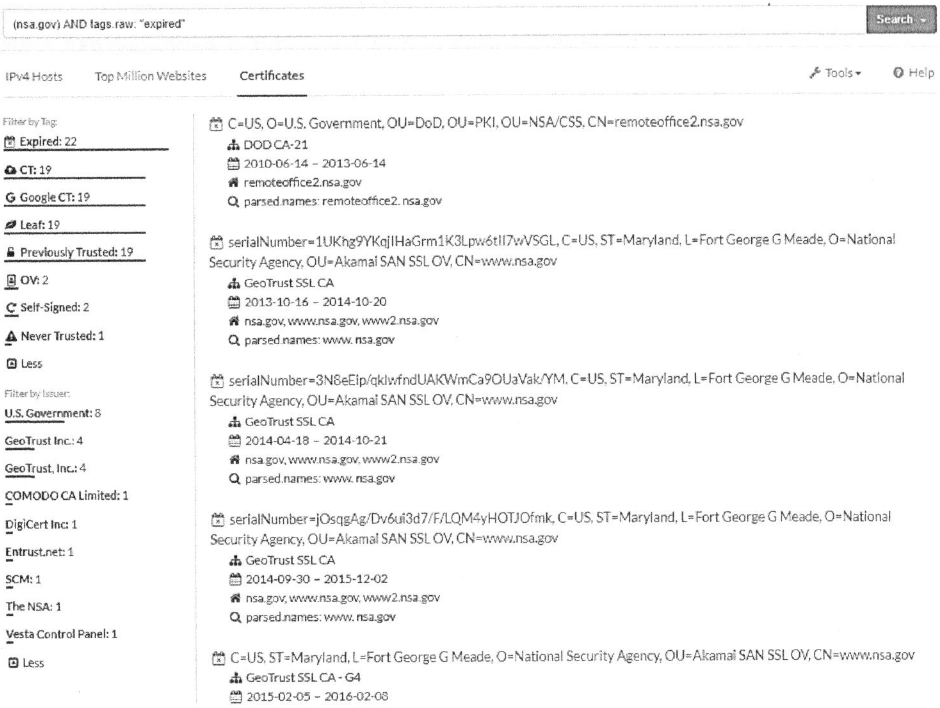

Figure 43 NSA.gov certificates (nsa.gov) AND tags.raw: "expired"

Also:

443.https.tls.certificate.parsed.extensions.subject_alt_name.dns_names: nsa.gov

Query Metadata

Your query (443.https.tls.certificate.parsed.extensions.subject_alt_name.dns_names: nsa.gov) found 221 IPv4 hosts.

Figure 44 Censys NSA.gov certificate names Metadata

Country Breakdown

Country	Hosts	Frequency
United States	205	92.76%
Netherlands	15	6.79%

Figure 45 Censys Metadata Country Breakdown of certificates with alternate DNS names containing NSA.gov

Network Breakdown

Autonomous System (AS)	Hosts	Frequency
AKAMAI-AS - Akamai Technologies, Inc., US	74	33.48%
AKAMAI-ASN1, US	62	28.05%
NTT-COMMUNICATIONS-2914 - NTT America, Inc., US	27	12.22%
GTT-BACKBONE GTT, DE	21	9.5%
TWCABLE-BACKBONE - Time Warner Cable Internet LLC, US	12	5.43%
LEVEL3 - Level 3 Communications, Inc., US	4	1.81%
UUNET - MCI Communications Services, Inc. d/b/a Verizon Business, US	4	1.81%
XO-AS15 - MCI Communications Services, Inc. d/b/a Verizon Business, US	3	1.36%
BTN-ASN - PCCW Global, Inc., US	2	0.9%
CMCS - Comcast Cable Communications, LLC, US	2	0.9%

Figure 46 Censys Metadata Network Breakdown of certificates with alternate DNS names containing NSA.gov

Common Tags

Tag	Hosts	Frequency
https	221	100.0%
akamai	217	98.19%
http	217	98.19%

Figure 47 Censys Metadata Common Tags of certificates with alternate DNS names containing NSA.gov

5.12 Discovering weak Kingdom of Saudi Arabia MOFA servers

Log into Censys.io Search in IPv4 for **"mofa.gov.sa"**

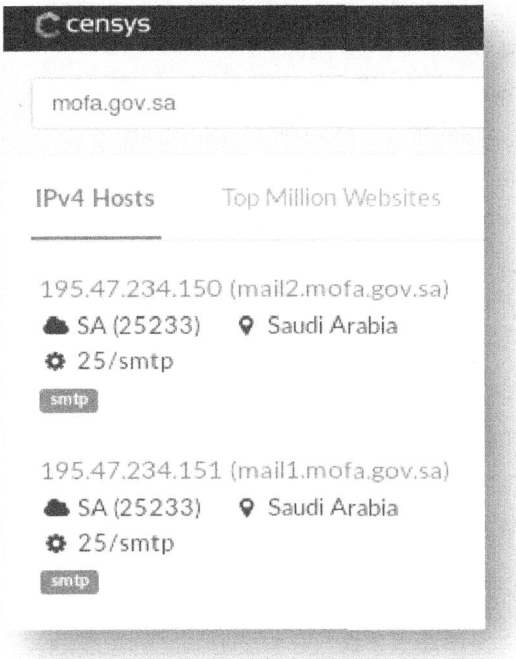

Figure 48 Censys KSA MOFA intelligence services search results

Select the first host and look into the port 25 SMTP protocol details

25/SMTP

Banner Grab and StartTLS Initiation

Banner	220 mail2.mofa.gov.sa ESMTP
EHLO	250-mail2.mofa.gov.sa 250-8BITMIME 250-SIZE 20971520 250 STARTTLS
STARTTLS	220 Go ahead with TLS

TLS Handshake

Version	TLSv1.2
Cipher Suite	TLS_RSA_WITH_RC4_128_SHA (0x0005)
Trusted	False: x509: unknown error

Certificate Chain

9566af258d3e5b2e252f9025b694573766f9bfc1390bdb37428796ccdcb2b9fa
CN=Cisco Appliance Demo Certificate, O=Cisco Systems, Inc, L=San Jose, ST=California, C=US

Figure 49 Weak Saudi intelligence services email server

Both of the Kingdom of Saudi Arabia Ministry of Foreign Affairs email servers were weakly configured in the same manner:

- Incorrectly configured with Start TLS email encryption
- Known, insecure RC4 encryption algorithm in use
- The encryption certificate is use is a Cisco demonstration certificate, which is supposed to be used only for demos or testing.
- The encryption certificate due to obvious weaknesses is not trusted.

The Saudi ministry of Foreign Affairs is essentially the intelligence arm of the Kingdom of Saudi Arabia, under control of MBS, the Crowne Prince of Saudi Arabia. MBS who's nickname is Teddy Bear, was in 2019 tied to the brutal, grizzly murder of the journalist Jamal Khashoggi. Turkish intelligence discovered the murder and made it public after the a series of Saudi MOFA fails allowed the actual murder audio to be recorded.

CASE STUDY: Responsible disclosure to the NSA

In the summer of 2017, Security BSides Las Vegas accepted a one-day training workshop I submitted. Called OSINT Crash Course for Hackers. Since it was Hacker Summer Camp, the pressure was on to build great training, one that would stand out from the conferences. I thought I would focus on intelligence agencies and government organisations to make it fun. When dealing with OSINT, timely, accurate information is paramount. Two weeks before the event, I carefully gathered together new research and built the final labs.

During all the research fun, using Censys.io, I discovered two vulnerable NSA.gov servers. Diffie-Hellman key exchange, a frequently used cryptography algorithm, found in HTTPS, SSH, IPSec, SMTPS and other protocols which use TLS. In 2015, researchers discovered weaknesses in the in the TLS protocol and how DHE is deployed, allowing encryption to be downgraded using a technique called Logjam Attack. The NSA servers were found using the domain NSA.gov and the tag DHE-Export. Any server supports DHE-Export potentially vulnerable. Exploitation was tested using a Logjam web-based testing tool which verified using the certificate properties.

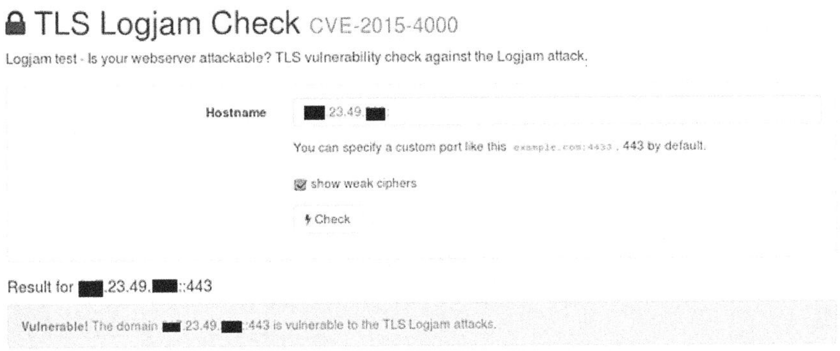

Figure 50 Crypto Log Jam Check positive vulnerability

CASE STUDY: Responsible disclosure to the NSA

After discovery, I was both happy but aware responsible disclosure was required. Not being a spook, I've got no formal relationship with the NSA, but I know people who used to work for them. Travel, life made it difficult, so I asked one of the people formally associated with the agency out for drinks and dinner the night before the course. Around 8 pm we looked over the findings, stressing I did not decrypt anything and chatted about the possibility they were old orphan assets forgotten. We chuckled a little arrogantly about vulnerabilities I found in other intelligence agencies.

The friend was very generous with drinks, threatening to turn night into day, so I headed back to be fresh for an 8 am start the next day to teach a full day workshop. By 1030 am the next day, my students went to test the NSA servers for Logjam, but they were no longer vulnerable, patched and reconfigured. It was the quickest response and least hassle responsible disclosure I've ever experienced.

Figure 51 Honest NSA Meme from LibertyManiacs.com

References

LogJam security vulnerability against DHE Export
https://en.wikipedia.org/wiki/Logjam_(computer_security)

Jamal Khashoggi
https://en.wikipedia.org/wiki/Jamal_Khashoggi

Chapter 6

Dorking with Censys

INFORMATION IN THIS CHAPTER:

- Why Censys Dorking is different
- Examples of useful Censys Dorks
- How to translate Google and other Dorks into Censys Dorks
- How to find entertainment via Dorking
- Case Study: Making Ministers WannaCry

Yet the deepest truths are best read between the lines, and, for the most part, refuse to be written.

- Amos Bronson Alcott

6 Dorking with Censys

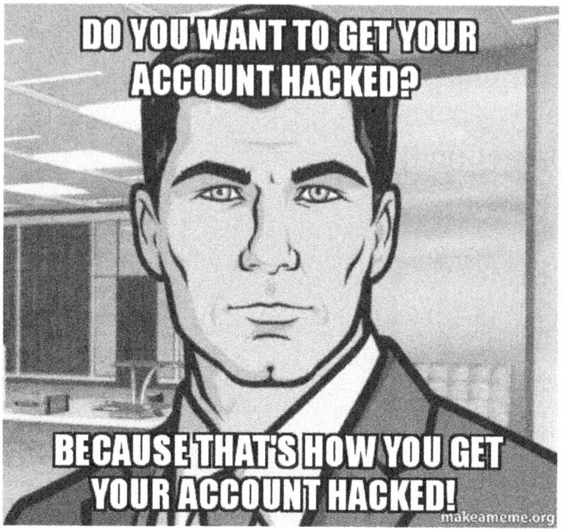

6.1 Introduction to Censys Dorking

Yes, you can use Censys for Dorking, similar to Google, DuckDuckGo, StartPage and other search engines. Many of the Dorks form the Google Hacking Database can be converted into Censys format. Dorking in Censys can get very advanced, and I could write an entire book only on Censys Dorking. The examples are for getting you started.

6.2 Converting Dorks into Censys Dorks

Looking through websites with dorks is somewhat easy. Censys scans HTTP website properties over ports 80, 8080, 8888, and 7547.cwmp.

Censys field	Example
80.http.get.title	Timeweb
80.http.get.body	HTML, JavaScript, body of a website
80.http.get.headers.server	nginx/1.12.1
80.http.get.metadata.product	nginx
80.http.get.metadata.version	1.12.1
80.http.get.status_code	200
80.http.get.metadata.manufacturer	Schneider Electric
7547.cwmp.get.body	HTML, JavaScript, body of a website
80.http.get.title	Apache Tomcat/7.0.28
Ports:	(80 OR 8080 OR 8888 OR 7547)
Protocols:	("80/http" OR "22/ssh" OR "7547/cwmp"OR "8888/http"

	OR "8080/http")

6.3 Discovering Porn websites

Pornography websites are businesses which must handle client data properly or risk losing customers and visitors. After a dating website aimed at having marital affairs called Ashley Madison was the victim of a breach. Porn websites, who already took security quite seriously; began bug bounty programs with good pay-outs. However, looking specifically for Bug Bounties is commercial use and requires a paid Censys commercial account. Using an IPv4 Censys search:

80.http.get.title: porn

The result finds some assets named or associated with PornHub.com

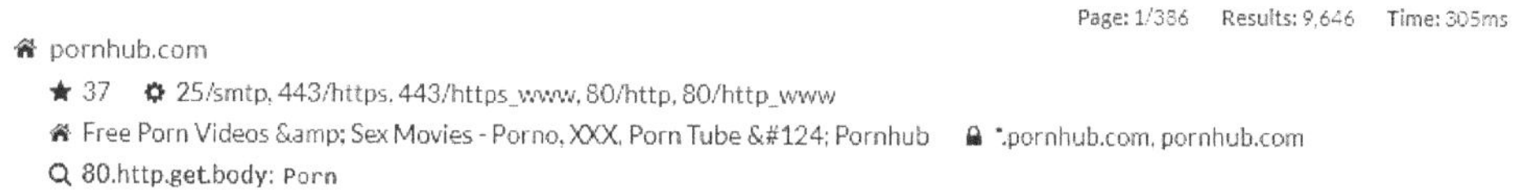

Figure 52 Censys keyword Porn Dorking

Looking further into the details, we want to find systems with a certificate for PornHub.com. Copy and paste the HTTPS information from one of the search results:

443.https.tls.certificate.parsed.extensions.subject_alt_name.dns_names: pornhub.com

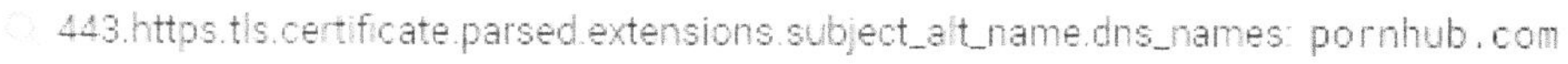

Figure 53 Censys HTTPS certificate DNS for PornHub.com

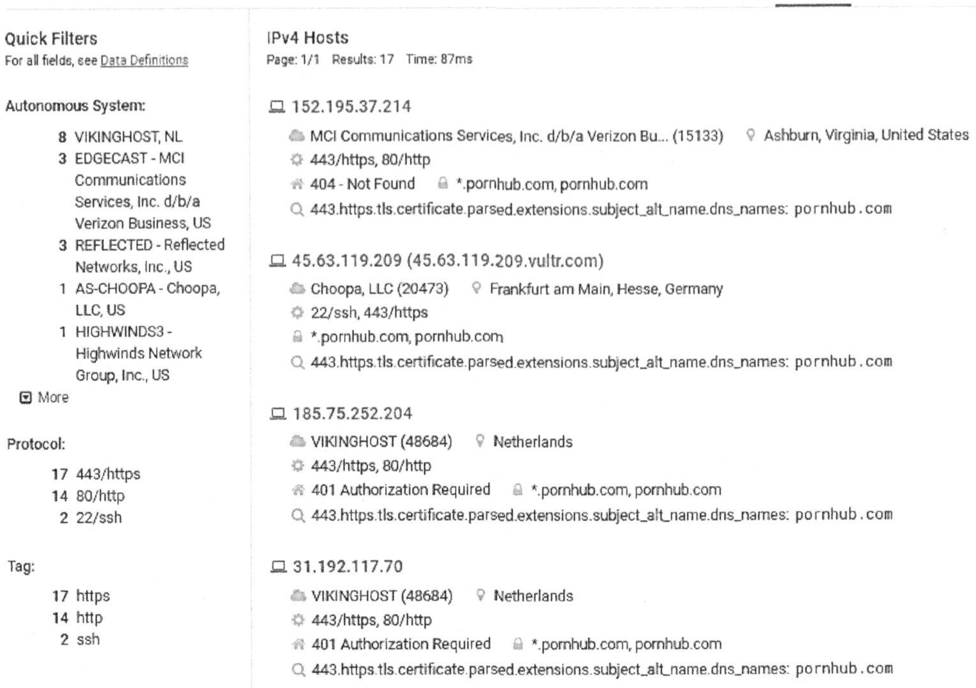

Figure 54 Censys web search result for PornHub.com DNS names in certificates

Next, click on the SSH Tag, then click the first host shown for details.

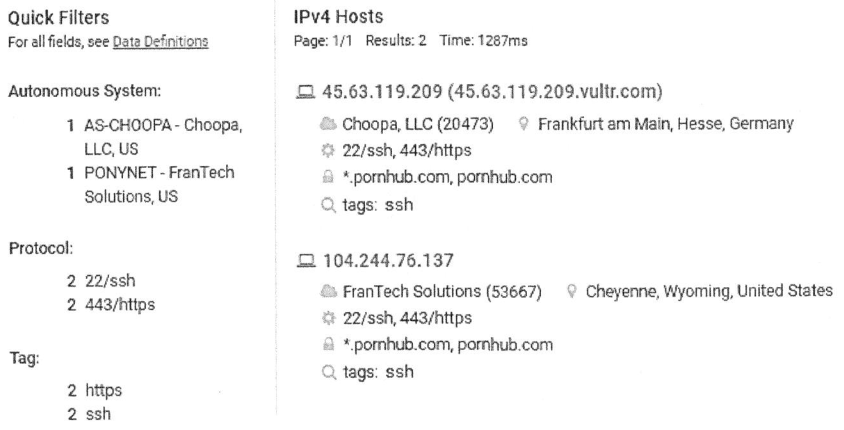

*Figure 55 Censys web search result *.PornHub.com SSH services*

Look for the **SSH details** and the version of SSH in use.

Figure 56 Censys PornHub.com associated system SSH details

Next, open a web browser tab and search, using your regular search engine. Look for any exploits or vulnerabilities for the version of OpenSSH in use. A good source for vulnerabilities and a listing of any related Metasploit modules is CVE Details at cvedetails.com

OpenSSH 7.4 exploits

Figure 57 CVEDetails result for OpenSSH version 7.4 vulnerabilities

6.4 Find Websites with Shells

This is a dork which is a play on a Google Hacking Database

Dork **80.http.get.body: "shell.php"**

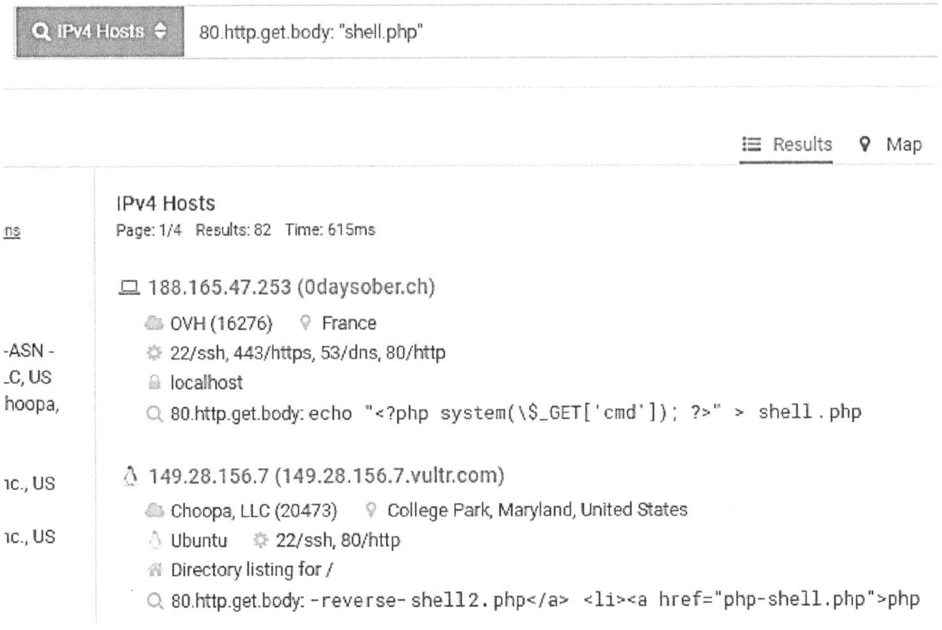

Figure 58 Censys search for reverse shells

6.5 Discover WannaCry infected systems

Many of the Google based Dorks in the Google Hacking Database can be rewritten to use with Censys. The database is an brilliant community tool, maintained by Hackers for Charity, a technology based NGO. **https://www.exploit-db.com/google-hacking-database**

When ZMap scans the internet, it can grab the HTTP/S headers, Body, Title and other fields which can be leveraged with Dorking. The WannaCry Dorks can be found in Footholds which are compromised/pwned or easy to compromise/pwnable systems. Using as an example Dorks from

https://www.exploit-db.com/ghdb/4489/

1. intitle:index of intext:@WanaDecryptor@.exe

2. intitle:index of intext:@Please_Read_Me@.txt

3. intitle:index of intext:wncry

Translating a Google Dork into a Censys Dork. Breaking down the first Dork: **intitle:index of** is the same as **80.http.get.title: index of**. There is an AND. The second portion **@WanaDecryptor@.exe** is in the text of the website, **80.http.get.body: @WanaDecryptor@.exe.** The IPv4 search string:

80.http.get.title: index of AND 80.http.get.body: @WanaDecryptor@.exe

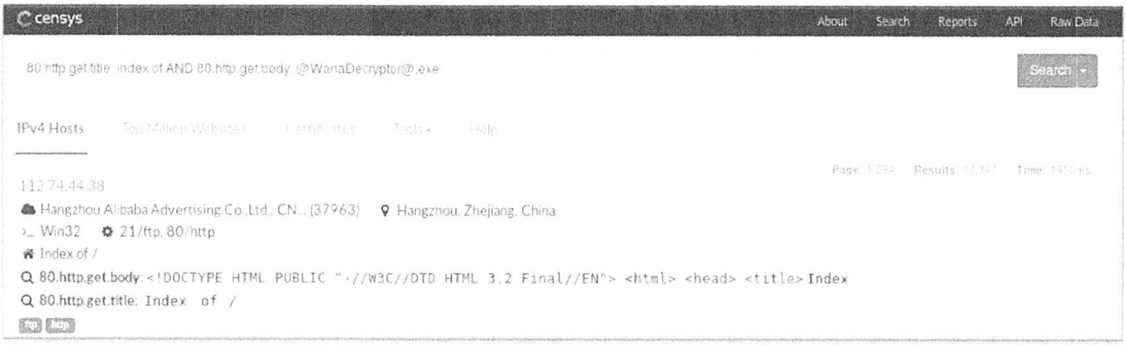

Figure 59 Censys search results for WannaCry infected hosts using Dorking

Figure 60 Example Censys HTTP Body field WannaCry infected host

6.6 Find Power Meters

Meter Net power meters can be discovered using a dork if they are connected to the internet and exposed. They have three main properties: Modbus, MeterNet in the HTTP title and in the HTML Body.

80.http.get.title: meternet

Figure 61 Censys Meternet power meter IoT login

Clicking into the details of the first system, then the Go button, the destination is a login page over HTTP.

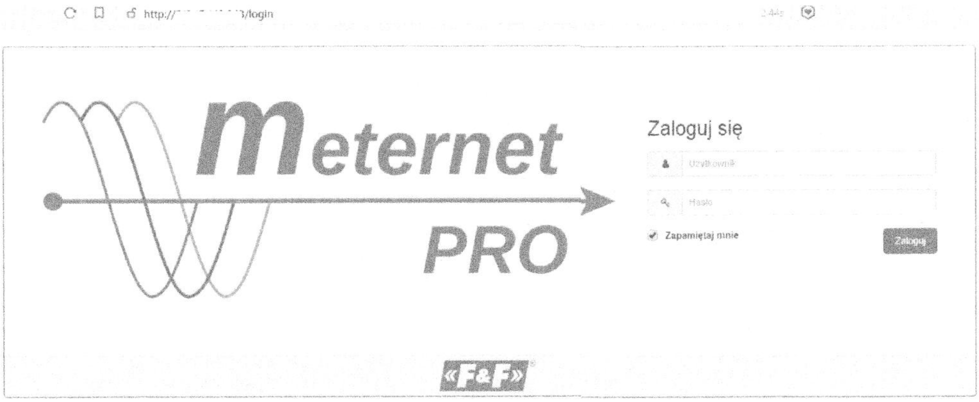

Figure 62 Meternet Pro system

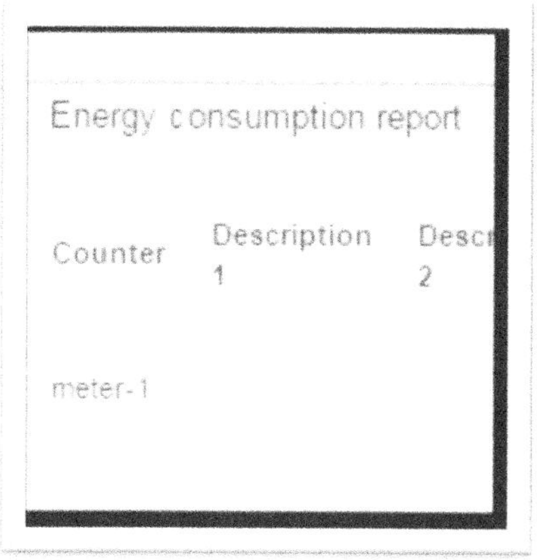

Figure 63 Meternet Pro access to picture files listed in HTML source code no authentication

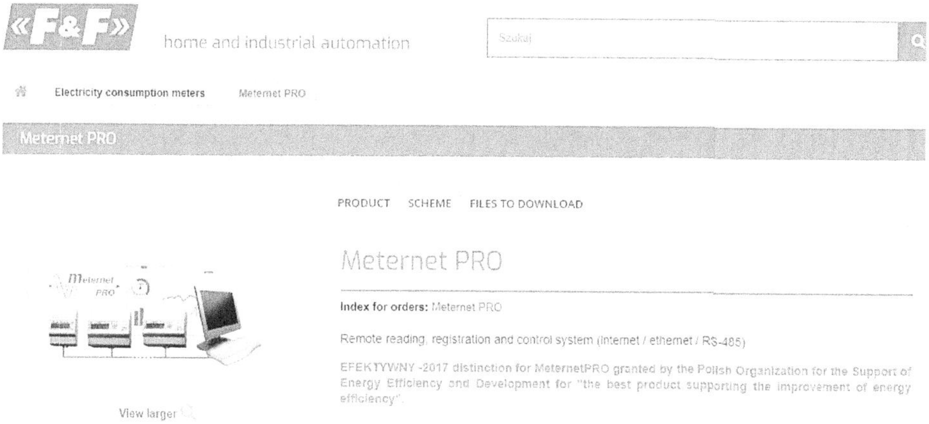

Figure 64 Polish to English translated website for F&F Meternet Pro

6.7 Find Procon LED Modbus controllers

Everything is IoT these days, even small LED controllers. Procon controllers are capable of performing additional functions beyond LEDs; this Dork should lead to other discoveries.

80.http.get.title: "Modbus to BACnet Configurator" OR 80.http.get.headers.server: "Procon Electronics Mod-Mux"

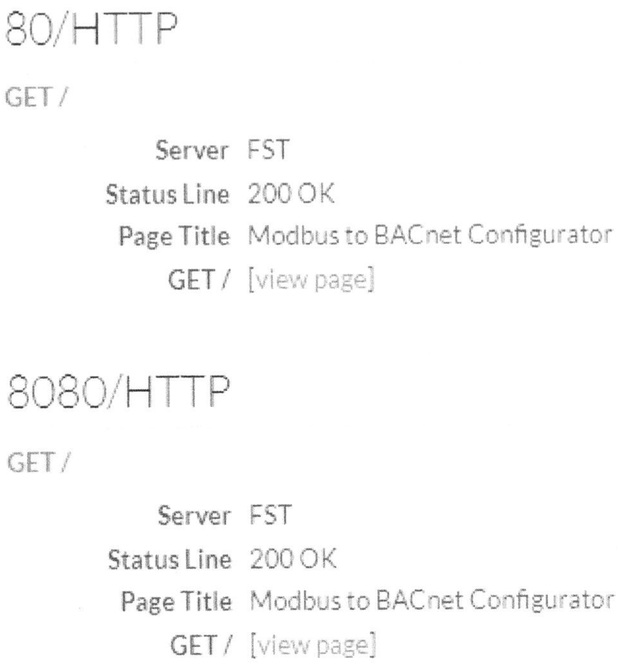

Figure 65 80 HTTP Modbus to BACnet Configurator

6.8 Find Samsung Web Viewer for DVR and Security Cameras

This Dork discovers Samsung branded digital video recorders which in many cases are CCTV. Many of these systems belong to businesses, governments and private citizens. The system can be exposed to the internet using a variety of ports which Censys scans as HTTP. Use the IPv4 search string, with all the various HTTP ports:

(ports:(80 OR 8080 OR 8888 OR 7547)) AND 80.http.get.title: "Web Viewer for Samsung DVR"

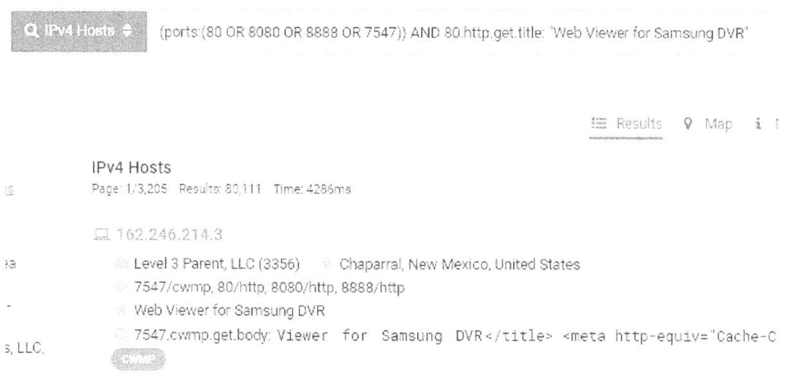

6.6 Dorking to find Anonymous FTP login services

There are many Censys FTP anonymous service dorking search strings which can be used in an IPv4 search.

- **21.ftp.banner.banner: "220 USE ANONYMOUS LOGIN"**
- **"ONLY anonymous access"**
- **220 Anonymous FTP Server**
- **220 Anonymous FTP Server ready**
- **220 (TK Anonymous FTP Server)**

A general search string which can be further refined:

protocols: "21/ftp" AND 21.ftp.banner.banner: anonymous

IPv4 Hosts
Page: 1/93,341 Results: 2,333,516 Time: 382ms

88.127.206.53 (izn33-1-88-127-206-53.fbx.proxad.net)
PROXAD (12322) Izon, Aquitaine, France
21/ftp
21.ftp.banner.banner: 220 Anonymous FTP server ready.

178.163.48.250
AS (8416) Tolyatti, Samarskaya Oblast', Russia
21/ftp
21.ftp.banner.banner: 220 Anonymous

Figure 66 Censys FTP anonymous FTP search

6.7 Using Dorking to discover Siemens systems

Censys scans the URLs of web pages where it can scrape this information. Using a dork from 2016 submitted by an anonymous person to the Google Hacking Database GHDB-ID: 4316, the dork will use the IPv4 web search.

80.http.get.body: Portal/Portal.mwsl

Contained in the 80.http.get.body HTML code is an a href HTML link to a URL with the matching properties.

```
"80": {
  "http": {
    "get": {
      "body": "<!DOCTYPE HTML PUBLIC \"-//W3C//DTD HTML 4.01 Tr
\n    <title>\r\n    SIMATIC 300(1)\r\n    </title>\r\n    <MET
  <body>\r\n        <a href=\"/__INTERNAL__Portal/Portal.mwsl?M
```

Figure 67 Siemens Simatic link in HTML

Another good dork is: **80.http.get.title: SIMATIC 300**

6.10 Find weak random number generator java.util.Random

Censys performs super-fast, in-depth HTML body scanning and

collects the results in its databases. In the OWASP basic security checklist for OTG-CPYPST, it stipulates initialisation vectors must be "random and unpredictable" with the example that java.util.Random is a "weak generator" versus java.security.SecreRandom which is stronger and should be used instead. We are going to leverage Censys' HTML body scanning and look for the weak generator in use across the internet.

Search Censys using the IPv4 option, looking directly for the weak random generator in the HTML body.

Figure 68 Censys weak java.util.Random search

Figure 69 Censys 80/HTTP system details with java.util.Random

The HTTP body will contain the Java package references using the weak java.util.Random. Using a find function in your browser will highlight all instances in use.

Figure 70 Censys html body using java.util.Random

CASE STUDY: Making Ministers WannaCry

Thanks to global warming, I was enjoying drinks outside with friends when I received a curious email from a top think tank. Did I want to present the keynote for EU and NATO member cyber warfare exercises in Brussels? After taking a moment to consider, about 30 seconds, I said yes. After final organisation and exercises were finalised by the Game Master Stefan Soesanto. Gleefully, I led the exercises after opening introductions by a technology partner. Twenty minutes, in front of Ministers of War/Defence/ State, Ambassadors and expert advisors. VVIPs big time.

The first slide was a picture of an internet exposed Chinese ICS SCADA system. Whilst I described how the Chinese government, through mandated certificate backdoors. Significantly weakened the infrastructure of China. Certificate management is difficult in a decent sized organisation. Imagine management but the entire country of China. Expired, weak ciphers, hacked, demo certificates are widespread. The Chinese government mandated they insert themselves on anything encrypted including banking, tax offices, production plants, hydroelectric dams, etc.

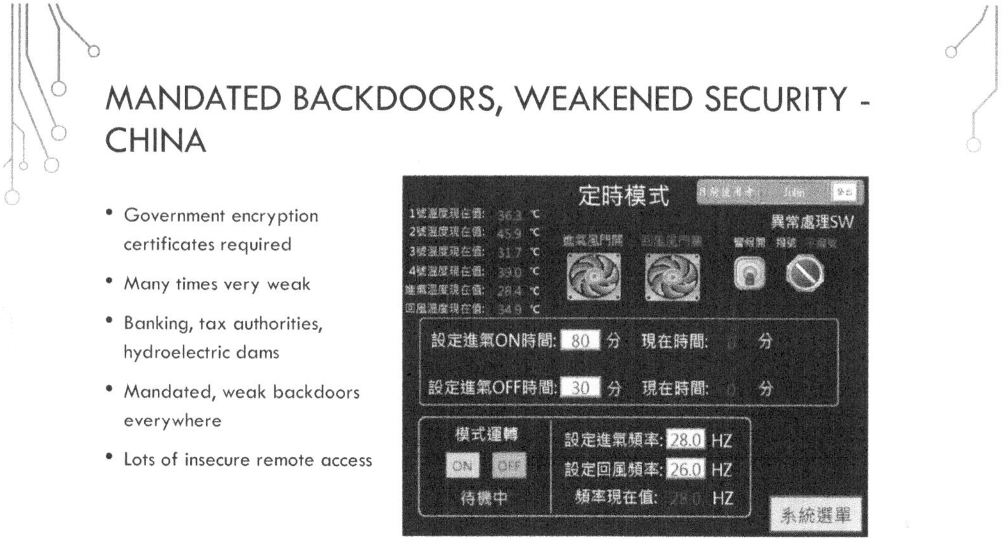

Figure 71 Weak Chinese encryption backdoors

The second slide contained pictures of exposed, weak water infrastructure in Europe and an ally country. There is a symbiotic relationship between water and electricity which makes them a primary target during a cyber war.

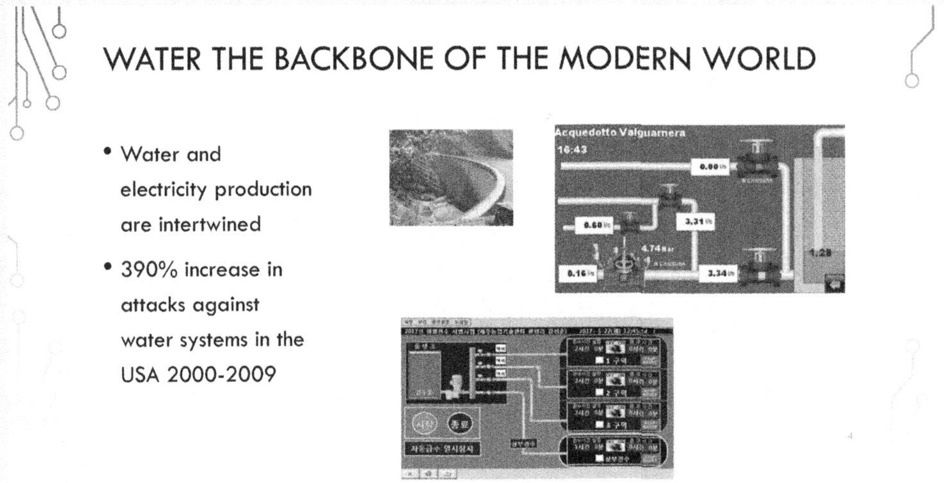

Figure 72 Weak water infrastructure

Figure 73 Shodan Modbus map exposed in the UK

Electricity and securing critical infrastructure is a matter of national and union defence.

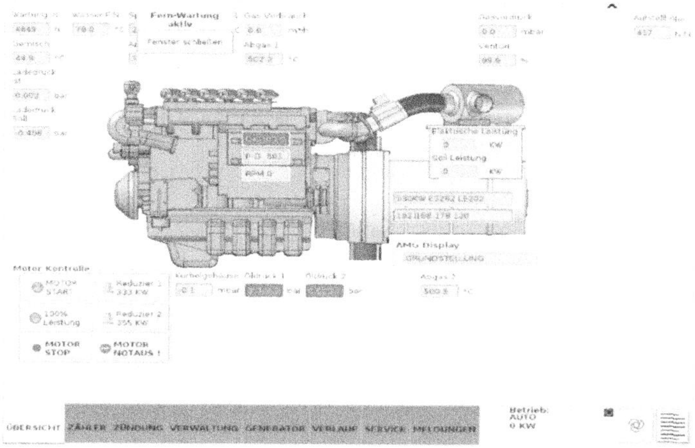

Figure 74 Exposed electric infrastructure

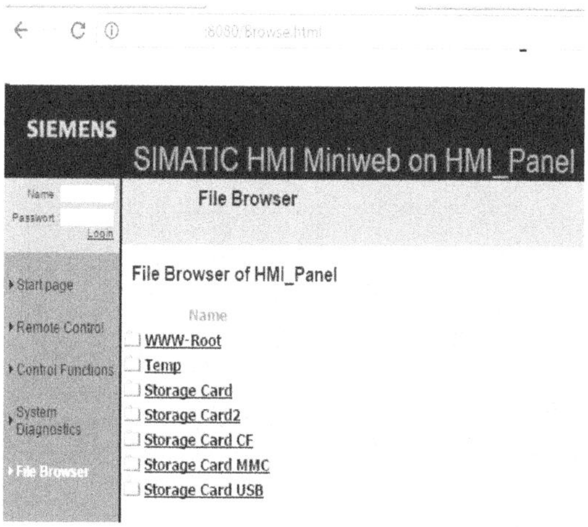

Figure 75 Exposed BlackEnergy vulnerable Siemens system

Systems which are vulnerable to WannaCry, but have not yet been infected. This is commonly referred to as a foothold. The risk is additional systems which could be infected and used as a bot network against infrastructure.

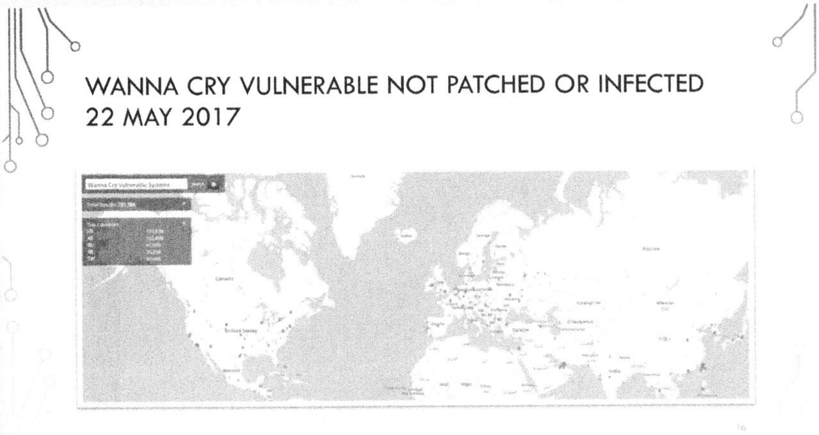

Figure 76 WanaCry vulnerable systems still unpatched

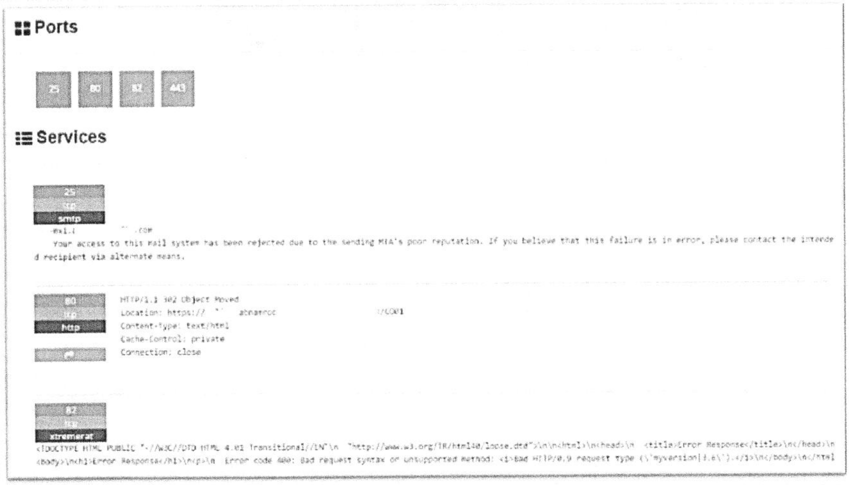

Figure 77 ABN AMRO bank part Dutch gov owned hacked with a RAT

References

How to catch a RAT at ABN AMRO Bank - Chris Kubecka
https://medium.com/@SecEvangelism/how-to-catch-a-rat-at-abn-amro-bank-5054e5a4799f

How to Start a Cyber War: Lessons from Brussels -EU Cyber Warfare Exercises – Chris Kubecka
https://www.youtube.com/watch?v=em1GObQAIOc

European Council on Foreign Relations
https://www.ecfr.eu

WannaCry ransomware attack
https://en.wikipedia.org/wiki/WannaCry_ransomware_attack

Marcus Hutchins (Some heroes have keyboards)
https://en.wikipedia.org/wiki/WannaCry_ransomware_attack#Impact

Chapter 7

BACnet, Modbus, DNP3 & Siemens S7

INFORMATION IN THIS CHAPTER:

- What is BACnet
- What is Modbus
- What is DNP3
- What is Siemens S7

Security is better when it's built in, not bolted on..

- Stephen Yu

7 ICS & SCADA

7.1 Introduction to Censys ICS & SCADA Protocols

Before embarking on ICS and SCADA related searches in Censys. It should be stressed, ICS/SCADA protocols, hardware, networks are not IT systems. However, there are some similarities, and many ICS/SCADA networks and production facilities use many IT protocols and assets. Early on ICS/SCADA protocols in general were analogue, using water, relay logic, serial connections, any engineering connection possible to drive automation. "In 1771 Richard Arkwright invented the first fully automated spinning mill driven by water power, known at the time as the water frame."

[12] **https://en.wikipedia.org/wiki/Automation#Control_actions**

Table 44 Censys 15/11/17 Host Report ICS and SCADA protocols

Protocol	Number	Percentage
MODBUS	26,128	0.01%
BACNET	16,519	0.01%
S7	4,524	0.0%
DNP3	357	0.0%
Total		

Add FOX

Table 45 ICS and SCADA Censys Tags

Protocol	Number	Percentage
MODBUS	26,128	0.01%
BACNET	16,519	0.01%
S7	4,524	0.0%
DNP3	357	0.0%
SCADA	71,140	0.03%

SCADA CONTROLLER	22,771	0.01%
POWER DISTRIBUTION UNIT	6,397	0.0%
SCADA SERVER	1,785	0.0%
SCADA GATEWAY	1,746	0.0%
PROGRAMMABLE LOGIC CONTROLER	1,135	0.0%
SCADA ROUTER	902	0.0%
INDUSTRIAL CONTROL SYSTEM	437	0.0%
SCADA FRONTEND	435	0.0%
SCADA PROCESSOR	56	0.0%

7.3 Exploring Modbus

Modbus is a protocol meant to be interoperable with a multitude of industrial electrotonic devices and programmable logic controllers (PLC). Considered a de facto standard and open source. Its significant limitations are the protocol standard written in 1979 when memory was costly. There are limited registers and addressing for devices. This can cause a lack of memory with return codes which make no sense. Modbus tried to update the protocol, with the introduction of ASCII MODBUS. This is considered among some engineers are bad For penetration testing purposes, the main issues with the protocol are it will accept any command, encoded, from any device, anywhere, without any authentication. The encoding is in Hexadecimal.

Chipkin automation books and website have a bevy of information, including tools for TCP/IP to Modbus, a Modbus scanner and other nifty tools.

https://store.chipkin.com/products/tools/cas-modbus-scanner

Table 46 Important MODBUS Censys fields & examples

Censys field	Example
502.modbus.device_id.function_code	43
502.modbus.device_id.mei_response.conformity_level	130
502.modbus.device_id.mei_response.objects.product_code	Anybus CompactCom Modbus-TCP
502.modbus.device_id.mei_response.objects.revision	3.05.01
502.modbus.device_id.mei_response.objects.vendor	HMS
502.modbus.device_id.support	True

Table 47 Basic MODBUS function names and codes

MODBUS function name	Function code
Read Coils	1
Read Discrete Inputs	2
Read Multiple Holding Registers	3
Read Input Registers	4

Write Single Coil	5
Write Single Holding Register	6
Read Exception Status	7
Diagnostic	8
Get Com Event Counter	11
Get Com Event Log	12
Write Multiple Coils	15
Write Multiple Holding Registers	16
Report Slave ID	17
Read File Record	20
Write File Record	21
Mask Write Register	22
Read/Write Multiple Registers	23
Read FIFO Queue	24
Read Device Identification	43
Encapsulated Interface Transport	43

Table 48 MODBUS Exception codes

MODBUS Exception name	Exception code

Illegal function	01
Illegal data address	02
Illegal data value	03
Slave device failure	04
Acknowledge	05
Slave device busy	06
Memory parity error	08
Gateway path unavailable	OA
Gateway target device failed to respond	OB

Function Code 91 = SemiSAN (Semiconductor Sensor Automation Network).

Per the Modbus protocol RFC, in the and device identification and user defined function codes "there are two ranges of user-defined function codes, i.e. 65 to 72 and from 100 to 110 decimal. Function codes and MEI Types shall not be part of this published Specification. These function codes and MEI Types are specifically reserved: 43/0-12 and 43/15-255."

Table 49 ZMap Modbus object mapping

Modbus Object name in ZMap	Required
VendorName	Yes
ProductCode	Yes
MajorMinorRevision	Yes

VendorURL	No
ProductName	No
ModelName	No
UserApplicationName	No

A tag based search, discussed more in the Tags chapter is:

(tags: "modbus") AND 502.modbus.device_id.function_code: "1"

7.4 Exploring DNP3

Table 50 Important DNP3 Censys fields

Censys field
20000.dnp3.status.raw_response
20000.dnp3.status.support
20000.dnp3.status.metadata.description
20000.dnp3.status.manufacturer
20000.dnp3.status.product
20000.dnp3.status.revision
20000.dnp3.status.timestamp

7.5 Exploring S7

The S7 protocol, which defaults on port 102. Is a proprietary protocol copyrighted and owned by Siemens.

Table 51 Important Siemens S7 Censys fields & examples

Censys field	Example
102.s7.szl.module_id	6ES7 214-1HG40-0XB0
102.s7.szl.support	True
102.s7.szl.copyight	Original Siemens Equipment
102.s7.szl.cpu_profile	China
102.s7.szl.firmware	32.81.37 28.01.2015
102.s7.szl.memory_serial_numer	04.18.2015 8SD23E
102.s7.szl.module	CPU 315-2 DP
102.s7.szl.oem_id	ControlBox V1.2
102.s7.szl.plant_id	City Nuclear
102.s7.szl.module_type	5478-FDC6-3B12-0E9A
102.s7.szl.reserved_for_os	IM151-8 PN/DP CPU
102.s7.szl.system	Integrated control system
102.s7.szl.serial_number	S Q-EOU022852010

7.5 General Siemens S7 Censys search

To perform a general sweep of Censys scanned systems using the s7 port 102 proprietary protocol. Then **Query Metadata**

protocols.raw: "102/s7"

Query Metadata

Your query (`protocols.raw: "102/s7"`) found 6,301 IPv4 hosts.

Country Breakdown

Country	Hosts	Frequency
Germany	1,065	16.9%
Spain	742	11.78%
Italy	617	9.79%
United States	524	8.32%
Turkey	389	6.17%
Poland	214	3.4%
Japan	186	2.95%
Belgium	176	2.79%
France	154	2.44%
Austria	148	2.35%

Network Breakdown

Autonomous System (AS)	Hosts	Frequency
DTAG Internet service provider operations, DE	746	11.84%
TELEFONICA_DE_ESPANA, ES	325	5.16%
VODAFONE_ES, ES	312	4.95%
TURKCELL-AS Turkcell A.S., TR	235	3.73%
CELLCO - Cellco Partnership DBA Verizon Wireless, US	191	3.03%
ASAHI-NET Asahi Net, JP	125	1.98%
ASN-IBSNAZ, IT	125	1.98%
AS3215, FR	107	1.7%
ATT-MOBILITY-LLC-AS20057 - AT&T Mobility LLC, US	104	1.65%
VODAFONE-IT-ASN, IT	90	1.43%

Common Tags

Tag	Hosts	Frequency
s7	6,301	100.0%
scada	6,301	100.0%
http	2,423	38.45%
https	1,257	19.95%
ssh	423	6.71%
telnet	416	6.6%
ftp	414	6.57%
embedded	284	4.51%
modbus	258	4.09%
dns	123	1.95%

Figure 78 S7 Censys metadata results

More detailed S7 102 dorking using the protocol fields itself can pin point systems directly. Using the IPv4 search function, look directly in the S7 protocol for Siemens.

102.s7.szl.copyright: Siemens

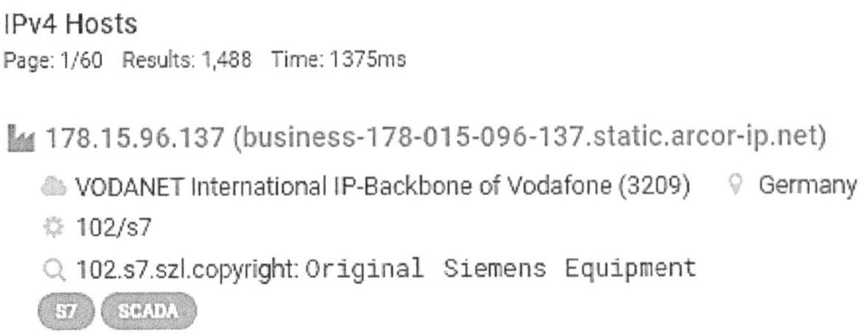

Figure 79 Censys S7 dorking for Siemens

7.6 General Siemens systems Censys search using certificates

Siemens does try to make some of their products more secure by using certificates. There are two quick dorks which search in the **Certificate** properties for Siemens.

parsed.subject_dn: siemens OR parsed.issuer.organization: siemens

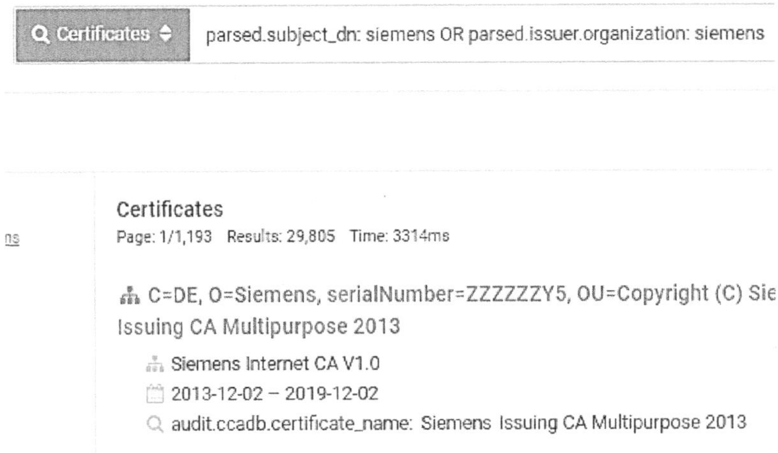

Figure 80 Censys certificate Siemens s7 with OR

Expand the Tags to display the certificate detail tags.

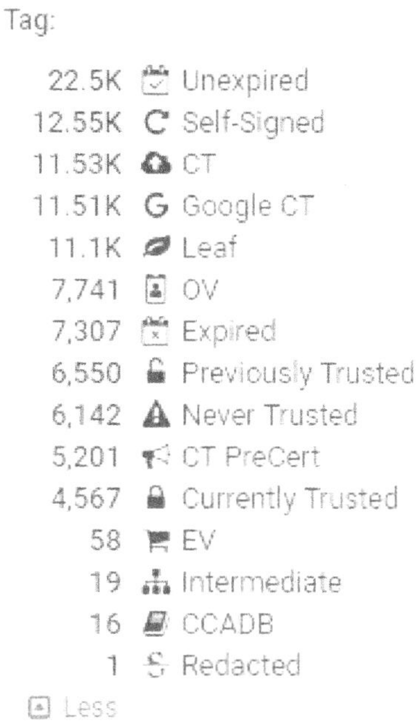

Figure 81 Censys certificate tags for Siemens

Further details about certificates use Tag properties which can use an AND or an OR.

tags.raw: "redacted"

(parsed.subject_dn: siemens OR parsed.issuer.organization: siemens) AND tags.raw: "redacted"

Never Trusted uses the tag "untrusted"

tags.raw: "untrusted"

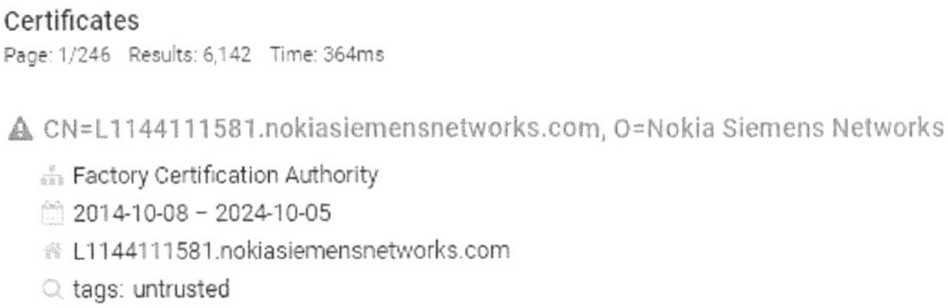

Figure 82 Censys Siemens untrusted certificates

7.6 Exploring BACnet

A protocol for building automation control networks. This communications protocol can control and exchange information between controller devices, heating systems, ait conditioning, water heaters, lighting, access control and other automation controls. Security was not originally designed into the protocol.

Table 52 Important BACnet Censys fields & examples

Censys field	Example
47808.bacnet.device_id.application_software_revision	Caverion\FI\Kokkola\KM_Kannus\AS01
47808.bacnet.device_id.description	VAK1 K-Market Kannus
47808.bacnet.device_id.firmware_revision	V2.5.1
47808.bacnet.device_id.instance_number	1025
47808.bacnet.device_id.model_name	PXC100-E.D + PXA40-W0 + PXX-PBUS / HW=V3.00

47808.bacnet.device_id.object_name	KMKannus'AS01
47808.bacnet.device_id.support	True
47808.bacnet.device_id.vendor.id	7
47808.bacnet.device_id.vendor.official_name	Siemens Schweiz AG (Formerly: Landis & Staefa Division Europe)
47808.bacnet.device_id.vendor.reported_name	Siemens Building Technologies

7.7 Find Siemens BACnet devices with web services

There are general survey two methods for discovering Siemens systems with BACnet. Using the Censys IPv4 search method:

1. **80.http.get.body: " 2013 Siemens " AND tags: bacnet**
2. **47808.bacnet.device_id.model_name: Siemens BACnet Field Panel**

7.8 Find OpenADR Management Interfaces

The Open Automated Demand Response (OpenADR) is a communications specification which can offer a certain degree of interoperability between different automation control protocols. Its backed by both NIST and NERC. The standard is accepted and in use in various phases in the USA, UK and China. Per the specification documentation, OpenADR systems should not be exposed to the internet as it offers no real security.

OpenADR protocol Interoperability

- BACnet
- Zigbee
- LonMark

OpenADR can control different types of devices.

- Solar inverters
- Water heaters
- Wind turbines
- Sub stations
- Smart meters
- & more

OpenADR also provides on demand responses during events between different components of the US smart grid. Load shedding and other electric balancing is also controlled by OpenADR. Per the related Wikipedia page on the implementation, key smart meter power pricing can be modified.

- PRICE_ABSOLUTE – The price per kilowatt-hour
- PRICE_RELATIVE – A change in the price per kilowatt-hour
- PRICE_MULTIPLE – A multiple of a basic rate per kilowatt-hour
- LOAD_AMOUNT – A fixed amount of load to shed or shift
- LOAD_PERCENTAGE – The percentage of load to shed or shift

For an operator to run and test the OpenADR software, there's an OpenADR Virtual Top Node which uses version 2.0 availible on GitHub. This software is never supposed to be exposed to the internet. The operating system is Ubuntu 14.04 or 16.04 with a MySQL database, Java, Apache , Torquebox, . The specification uses operator APIs, participant APIs and DRAC client PIS using a Rest API. There is support for TLS 1.2 encryption.

IPv4 Hosts

Page: 1/4 Results: 78 Time: 127ms

52[redacted]

MICROSOFT-CORP-MSN-AS-BLOCK - Microsoft Corporation ([redacted]) Québec, Quebec, Canada

443/https

hydr[redacted]openadr.com

443.https.tls.certificate.parsed.issuer.organization: `OpenADR Alliance`

Figure 83 Hydroelectric OpenADR exposed to the internet

CASE STUDY: Critical Infrastructure love ♥

The summer of 2012 reminded me of that Chinese double edged fortune cookie curse: May you live an interesting life. The world's most valuable organization was massively attacked with a phishing and malware attack. The company, Saudi Aramco, the malware Shamoon. Combine Arab Spring, Ramadan, a Wiper and >30,000 Windows systems inoperable and it was interesting times. Flame, another wiper hit Iran. Malware was slung back and forth between various Middle Eastern countries. With the involvement of various 3rd parties still questionable. For an in-depth interview about the 2012 Saudi Aramco attacks, DarkNet Diaries episode 30 **https://darknetdiaries.com/episode/30/**

The USA was not immune, experiencing a dramatic rise in critical infrastructure attacks. A natural gas pipeline company fell victim to spear-phishing. Allowing the attackers access to the critical infrastructure network. Internet exposed equipment management systems were targeted with brute force credential attacks, focusing on USA utility companies. Massive DDOS attacks against USA banks, halting services. Shook up consumer and government confidence in internet banking.

What is considered part of the USA National Infrastructure Protection Plan? "Chemical, Commercial facilities, Communications, Critical manufacturing, Dams, Defence industrial base, Emergency services, Energy, Financial services, Food and agriculture, Government facilities, Healthcare and public health, Information technology, Nuclear reactors, materials, and waste, Transportation systems, Water and wastewater systems"

An adversary can divert resources during an attack by targeting and exploiting multiple major points of entry at the same time. If the targeted nation has treaty obligations and an ally comes under cyber attack at the same time. It can further strain defensive and ultimately offensive resources. National level computer emergency response teams have an interesting role in keeping their constituent nations safe.

References

Critical Infrastructure United States
https://en.wikipedia.org/wiki/Critical_infrastructure#United_States

Darknet Diaries, Jack Rhysider, Episode 30
https://darknetdiaries.com/episode/30

Timeline Critical Infrastructure Attacks – Computerworld
https://www.computerworld.com/article/2493205/security0/timeline--critical-infrastructure-attacks-increase-steadily-in-past-decade.html

Modbus Application Protocol Specification V1
http://www.modbus.org/docs/Modbus_Application_Protocol_V1_1b3.pdf

BACnet
https://en.wikipedia.org/wiki/BACnet

OpenADR 2.0 Profile Specification B Profile
https://cimug.ucaiug.org/Projects/CIM-OpenADR/Shared%20Documents/Source%20Documents/OpenADR%20Alliance/OpenADR_2_0b_Profile_Specification_v1.0.pdf

OpenADR Virtural Top Node – GitHub
https://github.com/epri-dev/OpenADR-Virtual-Top-Node
https://github.com/epri-dev/OpenADR-Virtual-Top-Node/blob/master/documentation/1026755%20OpenADR%202.0%20Open%20Source%20Virtual%20Top%20Node%20Users%20Manual%20V3.pdf

Smart Grid OpenADR Implementations
https://en.wikipedia.org/wiki/Smart_grid#OpenADR_Implementations

Chapter 8

Solar panels, Alarms, IoT

INFORMATION IN THIS CHAPTER:

- Discovering smart grid elements exposed on the internet
- Internet connected fire alarms
- Internet connected entertainment devices
- Exposed laundry systems
- Exposed internet connected car washing businesses

If you suspect someone is following you, take four right turns. If they're still behind you, then they're following you.

- Creepy random internet person

8 Building Control Systems & IoT

Hey if it works!

8.1 Introduction to Censys Building Control Systems & IoT

Modern buildings can be complicated, requiring many different types of automated building controls systems. Lighting, climate control, hot and cold water, alarms, security, room automation, and more. The Internet of Things (IoT) can involve anything from solar panel arrays to a product which almost made it to market, the iCondom which was meant to record data about the size, temperature, thrusts and share securely to compare against other users.

Table 53 Censys 15/11/17 Host Report Building Control and IoT protocols

Protocol	Number	Percentage
DVR	136,600	0.06%
CAMERA	103,978	0.05%
FOX	26,232	0.01
RASPBERRY PI	24,092	0.01%
NPM	17,215	0.01%
NPM3	2,730	0.00%
SET-TOP BOX	2,460	0.00%
JACE	2,376	0.00%
HVAC	1,539	0.00%
JACE-7	1,437	0.00%
SOLAR PANEL	600	0.00%
ENVIRONMENT MONITOR	535	0.00%
JACE-403	535	0.00%
JACE-545	432	0.00%

TV TUNER	190	0.00%
TOUCH SCREEN	77	0.00%
LIGHT CONTROLLER	42	0.00%
CINEMA	29	0.00%
JACE-402	22	0.00%
FIRE ALARM	6	0.00%
Total	321,127	1.13%

8.3 Find Fire Alarms

Fire alarms shouldn't be connected to the internet with a public IP address, please don't do this. A simple Dork can be utilised with an IPv4 search:

tags: "fire alarm"

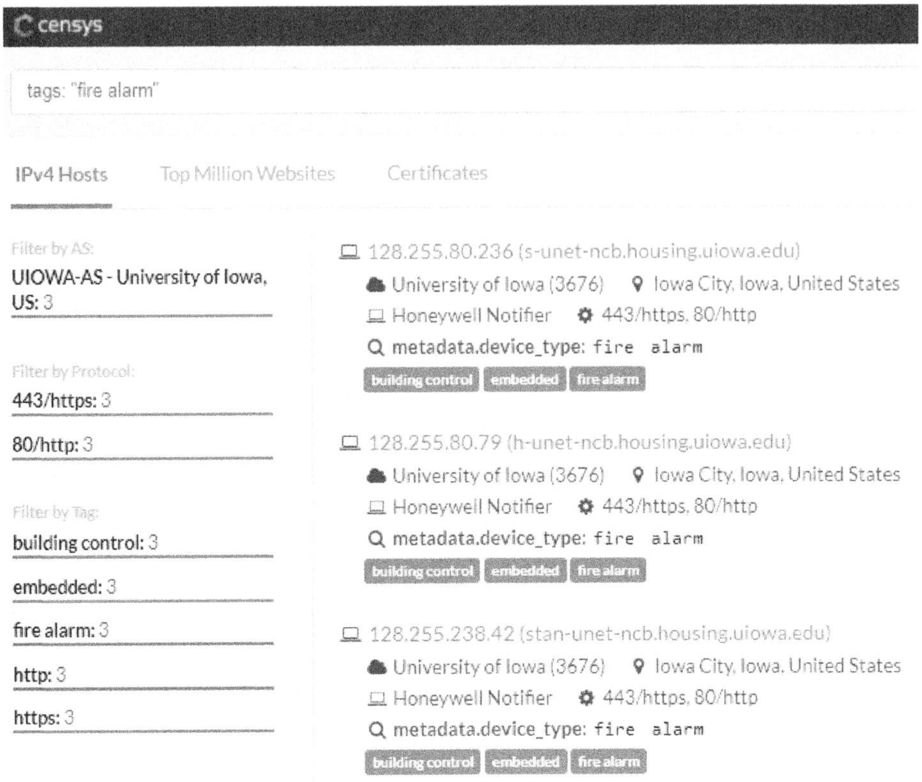

Figure 84 Censys Tag Fire Alarm web search result

Figure 85 Censys Tag Fire Alarm web search result detail

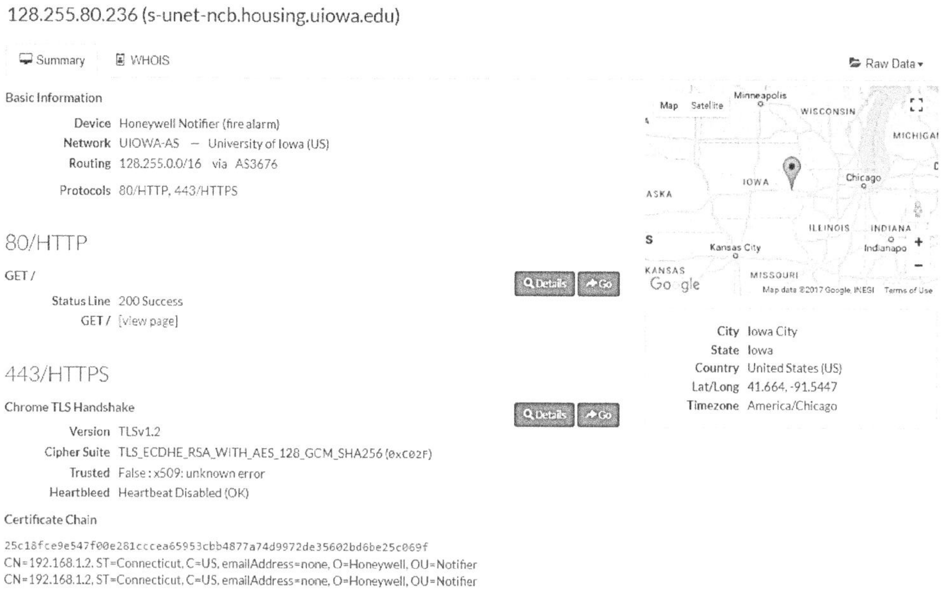

Figure 86 Censys web search fire alarm details page

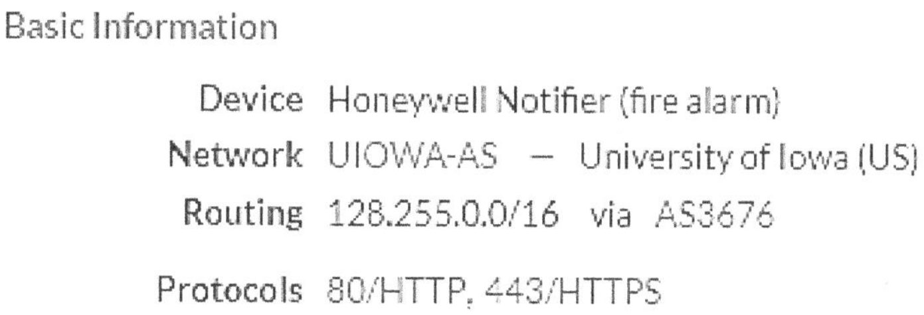

Figure 87 Fire alarm basic information details

Next, change the search string and click into the **Metadata** details:

443.https.tls.certificate.parsed.issuer_dn: OU=Notifier

Figure 88 Censys certificate OU containing Notifier

Your query (443.https.tls.certificate.parsed.issuer_dn: OU=Notifier) found 7 IPv4 hosts.

Country Breakdown

Country	Hosts	Frequency
United States	7	100.0%

Network Breakdown

Autonomous System (AS)	Hosts	Frequency
UIOWA-AS - University of Iowa, US	6	85.71%
ATT-INTERNET4 - AT&T Services, Inc., US	1	14.29%

Figure 89 Censys certificate OU containing Notifier metadata

8.5 Find Cinemas

Internet connected cinematic devices are exposed unnecessarily to the internet. Rarely patched, the firmware and software libraries left to decay. Leaving behind exploitable vulnerabilities which can be utilized for all sorts of naughtiness. In Censys web search, IPv4 enter the search string, then select **Metadata**.

metadata.device_type: "cinema"

Figure 90 Censys web cinema search

Country Breakdown

Country	Hosts	Frequency
United States	33	97.06%
Canada	1	2.94%

Figure 91 Censys cinema country breakdown

8.6 Find Solar Panel Systems

Solar panels are frequently connected to the internet so they can be remotely controlled. The easiest way to find solar panels is to search for them by the device type in IPv4.

metadata.device_type: "solar panel"

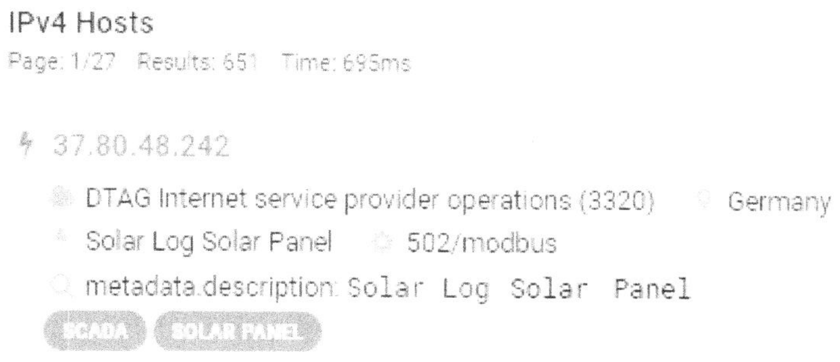

Figure 92 Censys solar panel device type search

Next, review all the **Tags** by clicking the **More** down arrow.

Tag:

651	scada
651	solar panel
622	modbus
358	http
248	ftp
49	ssh
29	building control
29	fox
25	https
17	NPM
13	NPM6
10	JACE
10	JACE-7
9	embedded
8	telnet
4	NPM2
3	dns
2	database
2	mssql
1	bacnet

Less

Figure 93 Censys solar panel device type Tags

8.7 Find Digital Video Recorders

There are multiple DVR manufacturers which jumped on the idea of the Internet of Things. As such, there are millions of possible DVR systems connected to the internet, mostly unprotected and rarely properly maintained with software updates and patches. Use the search string and variants to discover DVR players and systems. Some will be connected to camera and security systems.

80.http.get.body: "DVR Components Download"

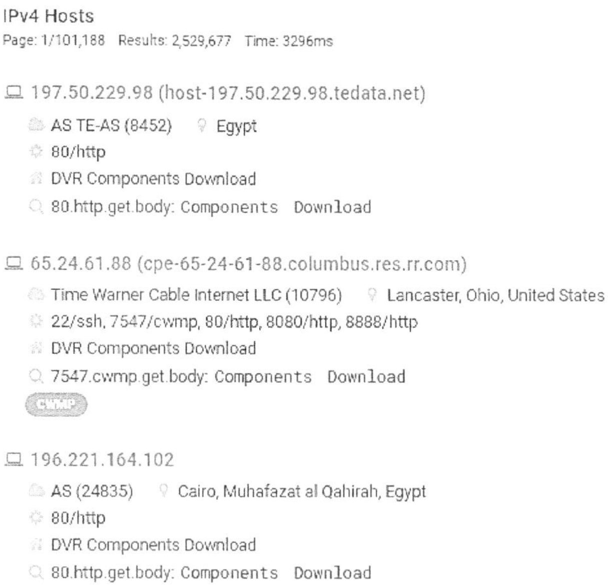

Figure 94 Censys Web Search for DVR Components Download

8.8 Find Miele washing machines & home appliances

Miele is a European home and commercial appliance manufacturer. From the lack of general security or essential OWASP Top Ten testing of their web applications. Its clear Miele focuses on appliance manufacturing. However, the organisation jumped on the IoT bandwagon, connecting their products to the internet and exposing their customers in the process. I've been trying to report issues with their commercial system web application and weaknesses in their payment systems. Sadly, Miele currently has no mechanism to report application vulnerabilities nor the appetite to seemly care.

If you have the desire or spare cash, you can buy a gateway device by Miele to connect your networked Miele appliances for about 399.99 GBP or $700. From smart energy systems to washing machines and dish washers. The firmware appears to be buggy per a blog post at **http://techblog.vindvejr.dk/?p=259** , and the release notes by Miele for updates are sketchy at best with " Stability improvements and bug fixing" is as descriptive as they get on the support page:

http://www1.miele.com/media/ex/int/service/downloads/xgw3000_release_notes.html

On a side note, if you have one of these devices. It appears the Wi-Fi modules on the Miele appliances have rather weak security. There's a tool on GitHub which allows you to interact with the Wi-Fi modules for testing and troubleshooting. To interact, the Group ID and Key must be used in the tool configuration. Luckily, per the instructions, this information can be sniffed and captured with Wireshark or any similar tool. **https://github.com/eikowagenknecht/miele-xkm3100w**

In the Censys IPv4 web search, enter the search term, then click the first asset which matches

80.http.get.title: Miele@home

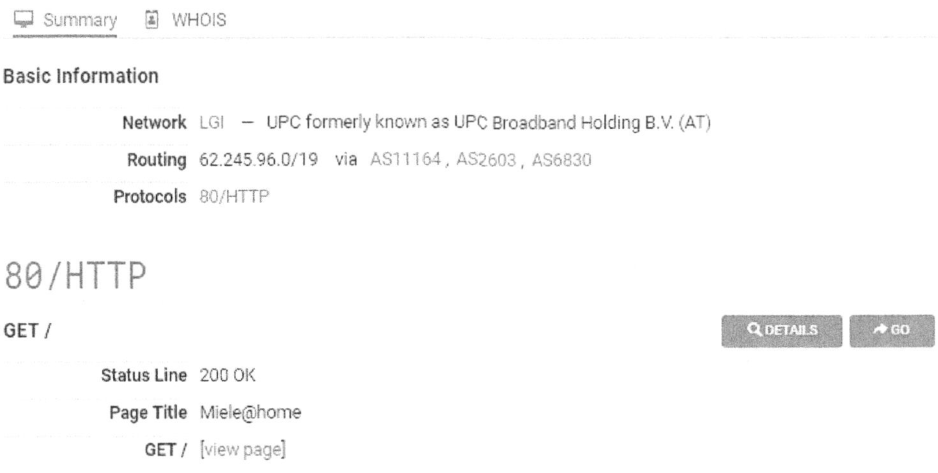

Figure 95 Censys Miele@Home detail

Now, go into the HTTP HTML details to verify this is a Miele gateway. Scroll below the table to the HTTP Body section.

```
<fieldset>
<legend>Miele@home Gateway XGW 3000</legend>
<table width="90%" border="0">
```

Figure 96 Censys Miele gateway HTTP Body details

What the home screen of a gateway device looks like and the login to manage the device. The login has a hard coded user name, which is the model of the device.

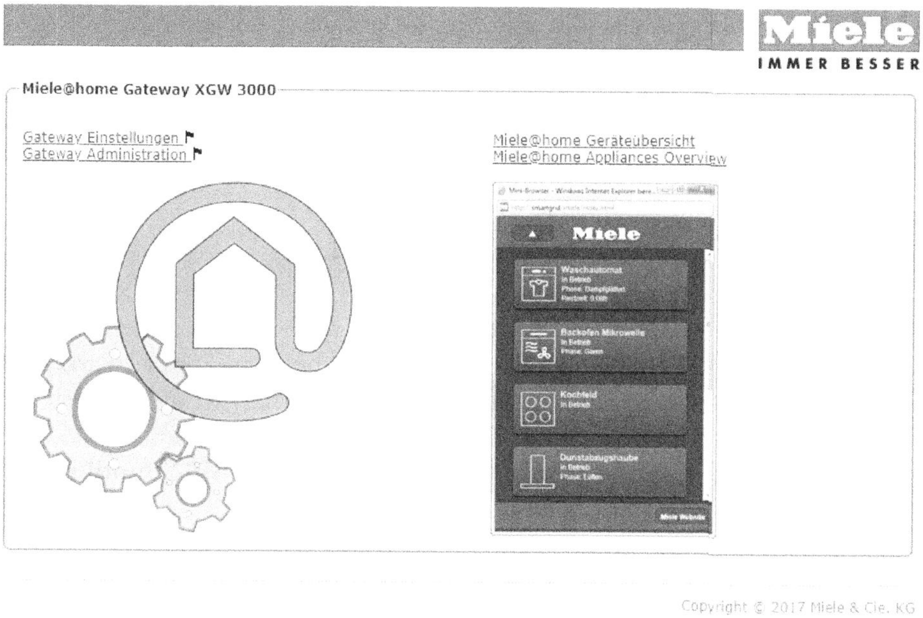

Figure 97 Miele gateway home screen

Figure 98 Miele Gateway Login xgw3000 is hardcoded as the user name

8.9 Find IoT Car Washing machines

This exercise can be accomplished in several ways. The dork is for a brand of remotely administrable, automated IoT car washers called Unitec. However, there are other markers to ensure they are the IoT/ICS SCADA variety we are interested in.

80.http.get.title: Unitec AND protocols: "502/modbus"

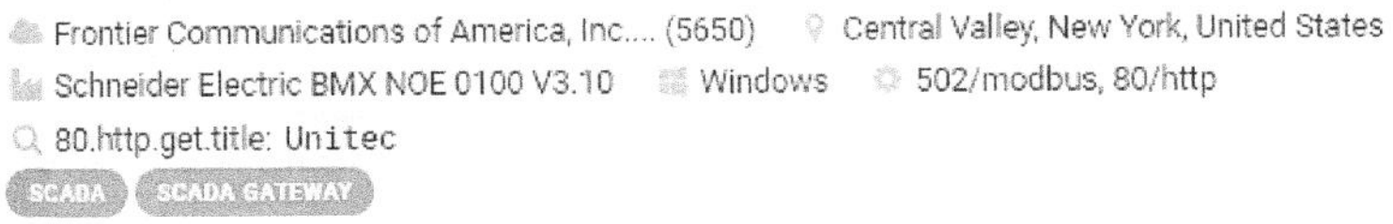

Figure 99 Unitec IoT automated car washers

Figure 100 Unitec web server details

8.10 How to Hack a Smart Home

If I had more money and wasn't so paranoid about IOT security, maybe I'd connect my house to the internet. These simple dorks will find the Loxone brand of smart home web interfaces. The web login can be on HTTP port 80 or other ports, such as 8888. Some versions of the web interface clearly were never security tested. Using the tool OWASP ZAP, I was able to find two directory transversal vulnerabilities which were exploitable and was able to bypass the login authentication with ease. I did attempt to responsibly disclose to the company to no avail. The version of the FTP Lexone uses is returned in the banner, vulnerable versions can be found quickly.

The web interface security content policy allows unsafe inline, eval, scripts to run.

```
<title>Loxone Smart Home</title>
```

/s

```
<meta http-equiv="Content-Security-Policy" content="default-src *; style-src * 'unsafe-inline'; script-src * 'unsafe-inline' 'unsafe-eval'">
```

To learn more, this Stack Overflow post explains volumes as to why this is insecure and not recommended: **https://stackoverflow.com/questions/37155270/content-security-policy-csp-safe-usage-of-unsafe-eval**

- **80.http.get.title: Loxone Smart Home**
- **21.ftp.banner.banner: Loxone FTP**
- **21.ftp.banner.banner: 220 Loxone FTP 7.0.8.17**
- **80.http.get.headers.server: Loxone 7.0.8.17**
- **80.http.get.metadata.product: Loxone**

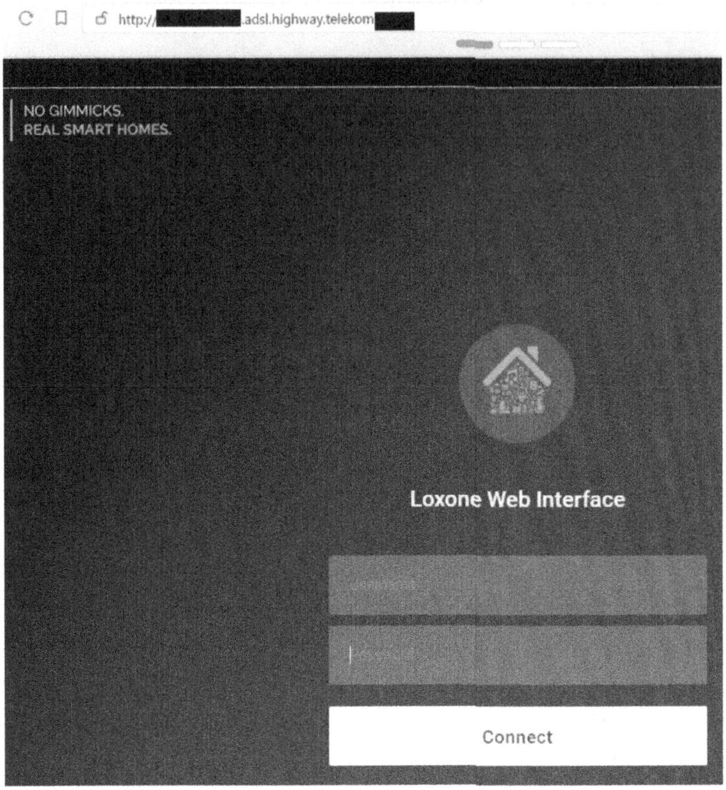

Figure 101 Lexone Smart House Login

References

Miele Brochures and Manuals
https://www.mieleusa.com/domestic/brochures-manuals-385.htm

Chapter 9

DNS & SMB & Other Protocols

INFORMATION IN THIS CHAPTER:

- Exploring DNS
- Exploring SMB

9 Other Protocols

Figure 102 AIBot Motivational statement

9.1 Other Censys Protocols

Censys and the ZMap project scan many protocols, report on most. Domain Naming Service (DNS) and Server Message Block (SMB) are frequently utilised protocols. DNS is a required service providing IP address to URL naming service. SMB typically doesn't require internet exposure. Both protocols can prove to be insecure depending on the version or the configuration.

Table 54 Censys 15/11/17 Host Report other protocols scanned

Protocol	Number	Percentage
DNS	8,866,809	3.89%
UPNP	1,820,000	Not included in Host Report
NTP	**Does not scan**	N/A
SMB	2,738,137	1.2%
Total	-	-

9.2 Exploring DNS

Table 55 Censys Important DNS fields & examples

Important Censys DNS field	Example
53.dns.lookup.additionals	ns1.afekv.com
53.dns.lookup.authorities	False
53.dns.lookup.open_resolver	0
53.dns.lookup.questions	{u'type': u'A', u'name':

	u'c.afekv.com'}
53.dns.lookup.resolves_correctly	False
53.dns.lookup.support	True
53.dns.lookup.additionals.response	54.210.13.81
53.dns.lookup.additionals.type	A
53.dns.lookup.errors	0 (false)

Table 56 Censys DNS Additionals fields

Censys DNS Additionals field	Example
53.dns.lookup.additionals.name	Keyword string
53.dns.lookup.additionals.response	Text
53.dns.lookup.additionals.type	Keyword string

Table 57 Censys DNS Answers fields

Censys DNS Answers field	Example
53.dns.lookup.answers.name	Keyword string
53.dns.lookup.answers.response	Text
53.dns.lookup.answers.type	Keyword string

Table 58 Censys DNS Authorities fields

Censys DNS Authorities field	Example

53.dns.lookup.authorities.name	Keyword string
53.dns.lookup.authorities.response	Text
53.dns.lookup.authorities.type	Keyword string

Table 59 Censys DNS Questions fields

Censys DNS Questions field	Example
53.dns.lookup.questions.name	Keyword string
53.dns.lookup.questions.response	Text
53.dns.lookup.quetsions.type	Keyword string

Table 60 Censys DNS Lookup fields

Censys DNS Lookup field	Example
53.dns.lookup.errors	Boolean
53.dns.lookup.open-boolean	Boolean
53.dns.lookup.resolves_correctly	Boolean
53.dns.lookup.support	Boolean
53.dns.lookup.timestamp	Date timestamp

9.3 Survey Chinese DNS systems

Using the Censys web search, use the search string or the URL, then press Metadata

tags.raw: "dns"

https://censys.io/ipv4/metadata?q=+tags.raw%3A+%22 dns%22&collection=

Figure 103 General DNS Censys web search

Go into the details for the country of China, the Censys web search string can also be used.

Country Breakdown

Country	Hosts	Frequency
United States	2,098,080	25.16%
China	1,986,789	23.82%
Russia	307,088	3.68%
Germany	236,118	2.83%
United Kingdom	209,553	2.51%
France	186,017	2.23%
Brazil	185,281	2.22%
Canada	179,616	2.15%
Turkey	174,734	2.1%
Republic of Korea	174,342	2.09%

Figure 104 Censys DNS China Metadata

Select **China**

(tags.raw: "dns") AND location.country: "China"

Next, add by using AND looking for DNS Answers Type A

((tags.raw: "dns") AND location.country: "China") AND 53.dns.lookup.answers.type: "A"

Select **Metadata** and review Common Tags

Common Tags

Tag	Hosts	Frequency
dns	1,541,310	100.0%
telnet	76,890	4.99%
https	54,916	3.56%
http	45,807	2.97%
ssh	37,778	2.45%
ftp	20,968	1.36%
cwmp	14,891	0.97%
embedded	13,795	0.9%
database	8,988	0.58%
network	6,600	0.43%

Figure 105 Chinese DNS Answers A Common Tags Metadata

9.4 Exploring SMB

SMB is a commonly used protocol, especially for Windows compatibility to share files on a network. US-CERT recommends disabling SMBv1 and blocking SMB at the boundary with no internet exposure: **https://www.us-cert.gov/ncas/current-activity/2017/01/16/SMB-Security-Best-Practices**

Table 61 Important SMB Censys fields & examples

Censys field	Example
445.smb.banner.metadata	Varies
445.smb.banner.smbv1_support	True

9.5 Discover SMB version 1 systems

The EternalBlue Double Pulsar exploit released by the Shadow Brokers utilised SMB version 1. Supposedly, the exploit was stolen from the National Security Agency's toolkit. After the exploit's release, it was repurposed for nefarious purposes. One of which was for the Wanna Cry mass infections that hit the world in 2017. During and afterwards, it was recommended to disable any instance of SMB version 1 and upgrade to version 2 or greater or switch to a different, more secure method of file sharing with Windows compatible systems. To find remaining, internet exposed systems still using SMB version 1, use the IPv4 search string, then click on a host, looking into the SMB details to verify:

445.smb.banner.smbv1_support: True

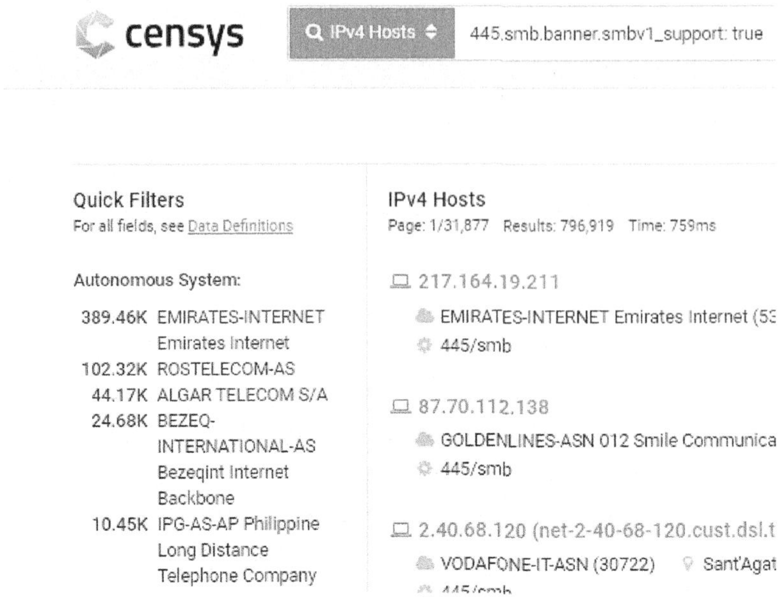

Figure 106 Censys search SMB v1 systems

Figure 107 SMB version 1 support is True

References

US-CERT Microsoft SMBv1 Vulnerability
https://www.us-cert.gov/ncas/current-activity/2017/03/16/Microsoft-SMBv1-Vulnerability

Chapter 10

Learning to love labels

INFORMATION IN THIS CHAPTER:

- What Censys Tags are
- Device Tags
- System type Tags
- Application type Tags
- Weakly configured Tags

The more I know about people, the more I like dogs. I simply like animals.

- Vladimir Putin

10 Tags

10.1 ZMap Project Tags

Part of the ZMap Project uses a component called ZTag, which combines

ZGrab output, raw scan data, and metadata to enrich device information. Searching by Tag is useful if looking for specific devices like **alarm system** which can operate on more than one protocol or port. Additional tags are added as the project progresses.

Table 62 Censys.io Tags

Tag	Description
akamai	Autonomous Systems on the Akamai CDN network
alarm system	Burglar alarm systems
bacnet	BACnet protocol detection
Broken installation	Detects server installations impossibly configured
building control	Devices and vendors identified as building control systems
cable modem	Cable internet modem
camera	IP enabled cameras
cinema	Home cinema systems
cwmp	CPE WAN Management Protocol
data center	Data center devices exposed to the internet
dhe-export	Diffie-Hellman Key Exchange Export Protocol
dnp3	DNP3 protocol detection
dns	DNS protocol detection
DSL modem	DSL internet modem
DSL/cable	DSL and Cable internet modem combination

modem	
DVR	Digital video recorder
embedded	Embedded systems with web servers
environment monitor	Temperature or other IoT environment monitor
ethernet	Ethernet device
firewall	Firewall devices
fox	FOX protocol detection
ftp	FTP protocol detection
Heartbleed	Checks the Heartbleed vulnerability status
http	HTTP protocol detection
https	HTTPS protocol detection
Hvac	Heating, ventilation and cooling systems
Idrac	Dell Integrated Remote Access detection
imap	IMAP protocol detection
imaps	IMAPS protocol detection
industrial control system	Systems and devices tagged as industrial control systems
infrastructure router	Telecom Infrastructure or similar
IPMI	IPMI Remote management detection
JACE	JACE protocol/ service

JACE-402	JACE protocol/ service
JACE-403	JACE protocol/ service
JACE-545	JACE protocol/ service
JACE-7	JACE protocol/ service
known-private-key	Reads SSL certificate fingerprint and checks against known fingerprints where the private key exposed, allowing decryption of any data
kvm	Keyboard, video and mouse switches
laser printer	Known laser printers
light controller	Light bulb and array controllers
modbus	MODBUS protocol detection
nas	Network area storage device
network	Network device
network analyzer	Deep packet inspection, network sniffer
NPM	Node Package Manager for IoT
NPM2	JACE-2
NPM3	JACE-3
NPM6	JACE-6
pop3	POP3 protocol detection
pop3s	POPS protocol detection
power controller	Building Management, IoT or ICS power controller
power distribution	Backup UPS devices

unit	
power monitor	Building Management, IoT or ICS power monitor
print server	Server which can share print services
printer	Any host with printer properties Brother, Cannon, etc…
programmable logic controller	Programmable portion of an ICS or IoT system which controls lower level devices such as sensors, actuators, etc…
raspberry pi	Raspberry Pi operating systems
remote access	Remote management applications
rsa-export	RSA Encryption Key Export
Running DD-WRT	Device with the DD-WRT operating system
s7	Siemens S7 protocol detection
scada	Supervisory Control and Data Acquisition
scada controller	Controller for Supervisory Control and Data Acquisition devices
scada frontend	Front end driver, front end processor/RTU for Supervisory Control and Data Acquisition
scada gateway	Gateway for Supervisory Control and Data Acquisition devices
scada processor	Report generation server for Supervisory Control and Data Acquisition data
scada router	Ruggedized routers for industrial and Supervisory

	Control and Data Acquisition systems
scada server	Integration of remote sites, different systems into a unified server for Supervisory Control and Data Acquisition
set-top box	Cable television access system
sign	Classroom and other connected signs
smb	Server Message Block protocol detection
smtp	SMTP protocol detection
soho router	Small office home office class router
solar panel	Internet enabled solar panel control and web servers
ssh	SSH protocol detection
strip-starttls	Detection of email servers which strip or remove opportunistic Start-TLS email encryption, which exposes communications to eavesdropping, spying and criminal viewing
switch	Network switch
telnet	Telnet protocol
touchscreen	Internet enabled touchscreens
TV tuner	Internet enabled digital television tuners
Update utility	Weak and detectable software update utilities
usb	Internet enabled USB devices and drives
VoIP phone	Voice over internet telephones
water flow	IoT base water flow controllers

controller	
wireless modem	Weak, exposed wireless modems

10.2 Alarm systems

Alarm systems can operate on multiple ports and protocols. However, most use HTTP or HTTPS and standard ports. Sometimes alarm systems are setup with too many default configurations or the vendor restricts the configuration, making it insecure. These type of conditions make alarm systems easier to discover if they are directly connected to the internet. Using the Censys web search, IPv4 with a tag search term.

tags: "alarm system"

The search will result in around 13,000 results. This is too much data, instead display the data in a different way. Go to **Tools**, then **Metadata**.

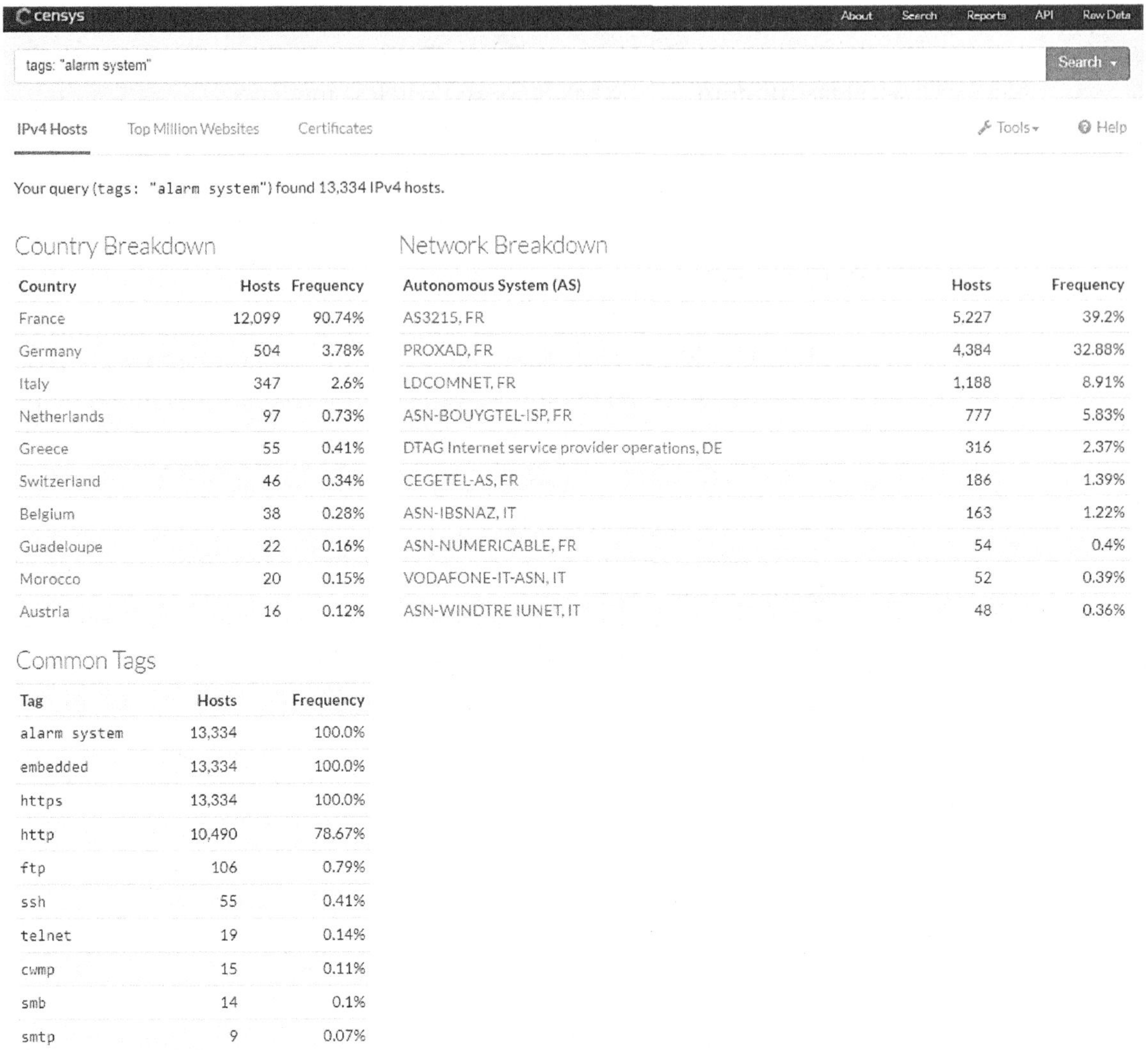

Your query (`tags: "alarm system"`) found 13,334 IPv4 hosts.

Country Breakdown

Country	Hosts	Frequency
France	12,099	90.74%
Germany	504	3.78%
Italy	347	2.6%
Netherlands	97	0.73%
Greece	55	0.41%
Switzerland	46	0.34%
Belgium	38	0.28%
Guadeloupe	22	0.16%
Morocco	20	0.15%
Austria	16	0.12%

Network Breakdown

Autonomous System (AS)	Hosts	Frequency
AS3215, FR	5,227	39.2%
PROXAD, FR	4,384	32.88%
LDCOMNET, FR	1,188	8.91%
ASN-BOUYGTEL-ISP, FR	777	5.83%
DTAG Internet service provider operations, DE	316	2.37%
CEGETEL-AS, FR	186	1.39%
ASN-IBSNAZ, IT	163	1.22%
ASN-NUMERICABLE, FR	54	0.4%
VODAFONE-IT-ASN, IT	52	0.39%
ASN-WINDTRE IUNET, IT	48	0.36%

Common Tags

Tag	Hosts	Frequency
alarm system	13,334	100.0%
embedded	13,334	100.0%
https	13,334	100.0%
http	10,490	78.67%
ftp	106	0.79%
ssh	55	0.41%
telnet	19	0.14%
cwmp	15	0.11%
smb	14	0.1%
smtp	9	0.07%

Figure 108 Censys Alarm System Metadata overview

Country Breakdown

Country	Hosts	Frequency
France	12,099	90.74%
Germany	504	3.78%
Italy	347	2.6%
Netherlands	97	0.73%
Greece	55	0.41%
Switzerland	46	0.34%
Belgium	38	0.28%
Guadeloupe	22	0.16%
Morocco	20	0.15%
Austria	16	0.12%

Figure 109 Censys Alarm System Country Breakdown

Common Tags

Tag	Hosts	Frequency
alarm system	13,334	100.0%
embedded	13,334	100.0%
https	13,334	100.0%
http	10,490	78.67%
ftp	106	0.79%
ssh	55	0.41%
telnet	19	0.14%
cwmp	15	0.11%
smb	14	0.1%
smtp	9	0.07%

Figure 110 Censys Alarm System Common Tags

10.3 Discovering Known -private-keys

There is a surprising and depressing amount of known private keys on systems and websites connected to the internet.

known-private-key	1,492,016	0.66%

Figure 111 Censys.io scan known-public-key tag results 15 November 15, 2017

Filter by Protocol:

443/https: 1.49M

80/http: 349.82K

7547/cwmp: 139.64K

22/ssh: 96.41K

8080/http: 94.88K

23/telnet: 69.62K

21/ftp: 61.48K

445/smb: 44.12K

53/dns: 37.39K

8888/http: 6,342

1900/upnp: 2,415

2323/telnet: 2,077

25/smtp: 1,583

110/pop3: 903

143/imap: 666

993/imaps: 338

995/pop3s: 238

1911/fox: 215

502/modbus: 119

47808/bacnet: 92

Less

Figure 112 Censys.io scan known-public-key tag Protocol Summary

Figure 113 Censys.io scan known-public-key tag and DSL/Cable Modem

Your query ((tags: "known-private-key") AND tags.raw: "DSL/cable modem") found 366,665 IPv4 hosts.

Country Breakdown

Country	Hosts	Frequency
Thailand	203,979	55.63%
Dominican Republic	84,246	22.98%
Spain	45,998	12.54%
Panama	11,731	3.2%
Ecuador	3,874	1.06%
Mali	3,603	0.98%
Peru	2,350	0.64%
Colombia	2,295	0.63%
Turkey	1,030	0.28%
Denmark	727	0.2%

Network Breakdown

Autonomous System (AS)	Hosts	Frequency
TRIPLETNET-AS-AP Triple T Internet/Triple T Broadband, TH	203,915	55.61%
Compaa Dominicana de Telfonos, C. por A. - CODETEL, DO	84,246	22.98%
VODAFONE_ES, ES	46,397	12.65%
Cable & Wireless Panama, PA	11,731	3.2%
CORPORACION NACIONAL DE TELECOMUNICACIONES - CNT EP, EC	3,874	1.06%
IKATELNET, ML	3,602	0.98%
Telefonica del Peru S.A.A., PE	2,350	0.64%
EMPRESAS MUNICIPALES DE CALI E.I.C.E. E.S.P., CO	2,313	0.63%
FPT-AS-AP The Corporation for Financing & Promoting Technology, VN	687	0.19%
KOCNET, TR	661	0.18%

Figure 114 Censys.io scan known-public-key tag and DSL/Cable Modem Metadata

Country Breakdown

Country	Hosts	Frequency
Thailand	203,979	55.63%
Dominican Republic	84,246	22.98%
Spain	45,998	12.54%
Panama	11,731	3.2%
Ecuador	3,874	1.06%
Mali	3,603	0.98%
Peru	2,350	0.64%
Colombia	2,295	0.63%
Turkey	1,030	0.28%
Denmark	727	0.2%

Figure 115 Censys.io scan known-public-key tag and DSL/Cable Modem Country Breakdown

Common Tags

Tag	Hosts	Frequency
DSL/cable modem	366,665	100.0%
embedded	366,665	100.0%
https	366,665	100.0%
known-private-key	366,665	100.0%
http	94,334	25.73%
cwmp	70,313	19.18%
ftp	6,209	1.69%
smb	3,795	1.04%
ssh	3,024	0.82%
telnet	2,459	0.67%

Figure 116 Censys.io scan known-public-key tag and DSL/Cable Modem Common Tags

Correct the tag
((tags: "known-private-key") AND tags.raw: "DSL/cable modem") AND autonomous_system.description: ""TRIPLETNET-AS-AP Triple T Internet/Triple T Broadband, TH""

To
((tags: "known-private-key") AND tags.raw: "DSL/cable modem") AND autonomous_system.description: "TRIPLETNET-AS-AP Triple T Internet/Triple T Broadband, TH"

10.3 Heartbleed vulnerable systems

Censys and its family of tools can identify and determine if a system is vulnerable to Heartbleed or not. The search term is a Boolean true or false.

443.https.heartbleed.heartbleed_vulnerable: True

Figure 117 Censys Heartbleed vulnerable search results

Country Breakdown

Country	Hosts	Frequency
United States	29,795	26.46%
China	9,842	8.74%
Germany	5,941	5.28%
Russia	4,549	4.04%
France	4,452	3.95%
Republic of Korea	3,710	3.29%
Japan	3,441	3.06%
Italy	3,217	2.86%
Canada	3,142	2.79%
United Kingdom	2,764	2.45%

Figure 118 Censys Heartbleed vulnerable Country Breakdown

Network Breakdown

Autonomous System (AS)	Hosts	Frequency
NOBIS-TECH - Nobis Technology Group, LLC, US	4,374	3.88%
COMCAST-7922 - Comcast Cable Communications, LLC, US	2,550	2.26%
KIXS-AS-KR Korea Telecom, KR	2,295	2.04%
CHINANET-BACKBONE No.31,Jin-rong Street, CN	2,270	2.02%
AMAZON-02 - Amazon.com, Inc., US	2,233	1.98%
OVH, FR	2,174	1.93%
AMAZON-AES - Amazon.com, Inc., US	1,681	1.49%
HINET Data Communication Business Group, TW	1,594	1.42%
CNNIC-ALIBABA-CN-NET-AP Hangzhou Alibaba Advertising Co.,Ltd., CN	1,580	1.4%
STRATO STRATO AG, DE	1,552	1.38%

Figure 119 Censys Heartbleed vulnerable Network Breakdown

Common Tags

Tag	Hosts	Frequency
heartbleed	112,623	100.0%
https	108,897	96.69%
http	76,162	67.63%
ssh	32,087	28.49%
rsa-export	21,048	18.69%
ftp	19,712	17.5%
smtp	14,897	13.23%
pop3	12,547	11.14%
imap	12,269	10.89%
imaps	11,987	10.64%

Figure 120 Censys Heartbleed vulnerable Common Tags

10.4 Find Russian FTP servers with databases

This search will use a protocol search in combination with geolocation and the database tag. In a Censys web search IPv4, enter the search term:

(protocols.raw: "21/ftp") AND location.country: russia AND tags: database

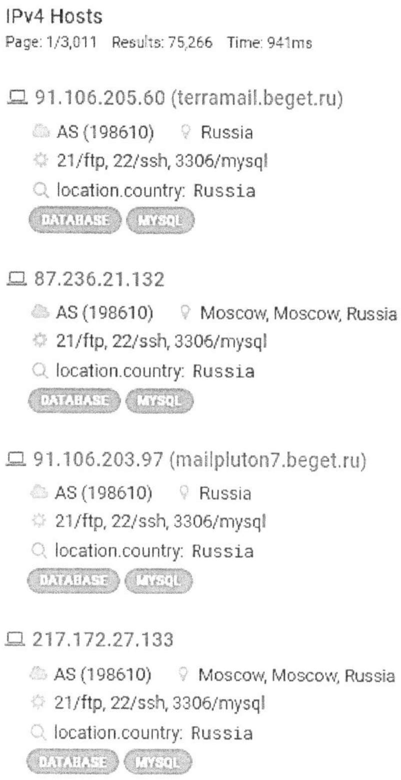

Figure 121 Censys Russian FTP database servers

CASE STUDY: Riding the Printer Pwnie

Discovering hackable printers with ease on the internet

Figure 122 Printers, a perfect attack pivot on your network

While researching this book, these lovely gems of printers began appearing in the search results. Censys.io is quite in-depth and also can apply Tags to devices or systems it finds. This nifty method can discover Brother or Dell re-branded Brother printers with the default web services enabled and the password never configured. A default insecure setup with no password. The internet always delivers. The world's most valuable commodity, printer ink, is at risk.

It's important to note, utilising Censys.io isn't the only method of finding these beauties. Vulnerable systems can be discovered quite easily using Dorking with Censys, Shodan, Google, Startpage, DuckDuckGo and other search engine scanning or indexing. Once the printers are found, the password can then be changed by an attacker over the internet or on a network, granting full control to an attacker. The printers can further be utilised as a pivot point to attack deeper into an exposed network by leveraging in-built Brother administrative tools. Brother was kind enough to build in some excellent tools for diagnostics.

Primarily, the vulnerable systems were found using the web-based interface of Censys. However, using the Censys Python library and API connection or one of my custom PowerShell tools connected to ZMap components. Additionally, tools such as Recon NG, Metasploit with Censys and Nmap scripts can connect to the Censys.io API key to more ninjafy other pen testing tools. Most of the printers host web pages on port 80, HTTP but some are on port 443, HTTPS. I used both ports in my searches and scanning.

Censys Dorking

If a password has never been set, several different models have a warning in the HTML body. Use Censys looking only in the HTML body, not the HTML title like in Google Dorking.

80.http.get.body

%22Please%26%2332%3Bconfigure%26%2332%3Bthe%26%2332%3Bpassword%22

Figure 123 Censys Dork to find Brother printers with no password configured

Using the report function with another Censys field, the 80.http.get.title. The models of the printers are returned in a Host Report.

80.http.get.title.raw

	80.http.get.title.raw	Hosts	
2	Brother MFC-L2700DW series	275	8.10%
3	Brother HL-L2360D series	114	3.36%
4	Brother DCP-L2540DW series	109	3.21%
5	Brother MFC-J5910DW	107	3.15%
6	Brother MFC-L2740DW series	103	3.03%
7	Brother MFC-9340CDW	73	2.15%
8	Brother MFC-J6920DW	73	2.15%
9	Brother MFC-J3720	68	2.00%
10	Brother HL-3170CDW series	66	1.94%
11	Brother MFC-J6710DW	65	1.91%
12	Brother HL-L2380DW series	64	1.88%
13	Brother HL-L2340D series	59	1.74%
14	Brother MFC-J4510DW	56	1.65%
15	Brother HL-L5100DN series	55	1.62%
16	Brother MFC-9330CDW	54	1.59%
17	Brother MFC-J4620DW	53	1.56%
18	Brother MFC-J6510DW	52	1.53%
19	Brother HL-5450DN series	50	1.47%
20	Brother MFC-J6520DW	49	1.44%
21	Brother MFC-J5320DW	47	1.38%
22	Brother MFC-L8850CDW	46	1.35%
23	Brother DCP-J4120DW	44	1.30%
24	Brother HL-1210W series	43	1.27%
25	Brother HL-L6200DW series	41	1.21%
26	Brother HL-5470DW series	40	1.18%
27	Brother MFC-J6720DW	40	1.18%
28	Brother MFC-8710DW	39	1.15%
29	Brother MFC-J2310	39	1.15%
30	Brother MFC-L5850DW series	39	1.15%
31	Brother MFC-9130CW	38	1.12%
32	Brother MFC-9140CDN	35	1.03%
33	Brother MFC-8910DW	34	1.00%
34	Brother DCP-9020CDW	33	0.97%
35	Brother MFC-8950DW	32	0.94%
36	Brother DCP-L2520DW series	31	0.91%
37	Brother MFC-L2720DW series	29	0.85%
38	Brother MFC-J2720	28	0.82%
39	Brother MFC-J4420DW	28	0.82%
40	Brother MFC-J5620DW	28	0.82%
41	Brother DCP-1610W series	27	0.80%
42	Brother HL-3140CW series	27	0.80%
43	Brother MFC-J5720DW	27	0.80%
44	Brother MFC-J5830DW	25	0.74%
45	Brother MFC-L5900DW series	24	0.71%
46	Brother HL-L8350CDW series	22	0.65%
47	Brother MFC-L2700DN series	22	0.65%
48	Brother DCP-J4110DW	21	0.62%
49	Brother MFC-J6910DW	21	0.62%
50	Brother MFC-J3520	20	0.59%
51	Brother MFC-J4410DW	20	0.59%
52	*Other*	861	25.35%
53	**Total**	**3,396**	**100.00%**

Figure 124 Over three thousand printers with model :)

Connecting and controlling printers via the administrative tool

Brother has a fantastic little Admin application, updated in 2017. It can discover any Brother printer on the list you provide. Once the tool finds a compatible Brother printer, no password or login is required to connect. A local test printer is first one. The two others discovered via the Censys dork. Put in the IP address, range, it scans, and whatever it finds it connects to. The things one can do if they were evil. This tool gives a fantastic level of access, making it a dual use piece of software. Allowing it to be used for good and evil 😈

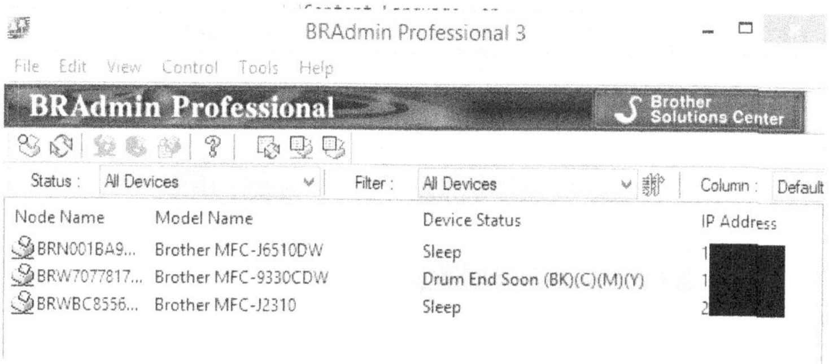

Figure 125 Even tells you the status, sweet

Compatible Brother tool models

ADS-1100W, ADS-1600W, ADS-2400N, ADS-2600W, ADS-2600We, ADS-2800W, ADS-3000N, ADS-3600W, DCP-1610W, DCP-1610WE, DCP-1610WR, DCP-1612W, DCP-1612WE, DCP-1612WR, DCP-1622WE, DCP-365CN, DCP-373CW, DCP-375CW, DCP-377CW, DCP-395CN, DCP-585CW, DCP-6690CW, DCP-7045N, DCP-7045NR, DCP-7055W, DCP-7055WR, DCP-7057WR, DCP-7065DN, DCP-7065DNR, DCP-7070DW, DCP-7070DWR, DCP-8085DN, DCP-8110DN, DCP-8250DN, DCP-9010CN, DCP-9015CDW, DCP-9017CDW, DCP-9020CDW, DCP-9022CDW, DCP-9055CDN, DCP-9270CDN, DCP-J105, DCP-J132W, DCP-J140W, DCP-J152W, DCP-J172W, DCP-J315W, DCP-J4110DW, DCP-J4120DW, DCP-J515W, DCP-J525W, DCP-J552DW, DCP-J562DW, DCP-J715W, DCP-J725DW, DCP-J752DW, DCP-J772DW, DCP-J774DW, DCP-J785DW, DCP-J925DW, DCP-L2520DW, DCP-L2520DWR, DCP-L2530DW, DCP-L2537DW, DCP-L2540DN, DCP-L2540DNR, DCP-L2550DN, DCP-L2560DW, DCP-L2560DWR, DCP-L5500DN, DCP-L6600DW, DCP-L8400CDN, DCP-L8410CDW, DCP-L8450CDW, DCP-T500W, DCP-T700W, HL-1210W, HL-1210WE, HL-1210WR, HL-1212W, HL-1212WE, HL-1212WR, HL-1222WE, HL-2135W, HL-2150N, HL-2150NR, HL-2170W, HL-2170WR, HL-2250DN, HL-2250DNR, HL-2270DW, HL-3040CN, HL-3070CW, HL-3140CW, HL-3142CW, HL-3150CDW, HL-3152CDW, HL-3170CDW, HL-3172CDW, HL-4140CN, HL-4150CDN, HL-4570CDW, HL-4570CDWT, HL-5350DN, HL-5370DW, HL-5380DN, HL-5450DN, HL-5450DNT, HL-5470DW, HL-6180DW, HL-6180DWT, HL-L2340DW, HL-L2340DWR, HL-L2350DW, HL-L2360DN, HL-L2360DNR, HL-L2365DW, HL-L2365DWR, HL-L2370DN, HL-L2375DW, HL-L5100DN(T), HL-L5200DW(T), HL-L6250DN, HL-L6300DW(T), HL-L6400DW(T), HL-L8250CDN, HL-L8260CDW, HL-L8350CDW, HL-L8360CDW, HL-L9200CDWT, HL-L9300CDW(TT), HL-L9310CDW(T), HL-S7000DN, MFC-1910W, MFC-1910WE, MFC-1912WR, MFC-255CW, MFC-257CW, MFC-295CN, MFC-490CW, MFC-5490CN, MFC-5890CN, MFC-5895CW, MFC-6490CW, MFC-6890CDW, MFC-7360N, MFC-7360NR, MFC-7440N, MFC-7440NR, MFC-7460DN, MFC-7840W, MFC-7840WR, MFC-7860DW, MFC-7860DWR, MFC-790CW, MFC-795CW, MFC-8370DN, MFC-8380DN, MFC-8510DN, MFC-8520DN, MFC-8880DN, MFC-8890DW, MFC-8950DW, MFC-8950DWT, MFC-9120CN, MFC-9140CDN, MFC-9142CDN, MFC-9320CW, MFC-9330CDW, MFC-9332CDW, MFC-9340CDW, MFC-9342CDW, MFC-9460CDN, MFC-9465CDN, MFC-990CW, MFC-9970CDW, MFC-J200, MFC-J2310, MFC-J2320, MFC-J2330DW, MFC-J2510, MFC-J265W, MFC-J2720, MFC-J3520, MFC-J3530DW, MFC-J3720, MFC-J3930DW, MFC-J415W, MFC-J430W, MFC-J4410DW, MFC-J4420DW, MFC-J4510DW, MFC-J4610DW, MFC-J4620DW, MFC-J4625DW, MFC-J470DW, MFC-J4710DW, MFC-J480DW, MFC-J5320DW, MFC-J5330DW, MFC-J5335DW, MFC-J5620DW, MFC-J5625DW, MFC-J5720DW, MFC-J5730DW, MFC-J5910DW, MFC-J5920DW, MFC-J5930DW, MFC-J615W, MFC-J625DW, MFC-J650DW, MFC-J6510DW, MFC-J6520DW, MFC-J6530DW, MFC-J6710DW, MFC-J6720DW, MFC-J680DW, MFC-J6910DW, MFC-J6920DW, MFC-J6925DW, MFC-J6930DW, MFC-J6935DW, MFC-J825DW, MFC-J870DW, MFC-J880DW, MFC-J890DW, MFC-J895DW, MFC-J985DW, MFC-L2700DN, MFC-L2700DNR, MFC-L2700DW, MFC-L2700DWR, MFC-L2710DN, MFC-L2710DW, MFC-L2720DW, MFC-L2720DWR, MFC-L2730DW, MFC-L2740DW, MFC-L2740DWR, MFC-L2750DW, MFC-L5700DN, MFC-L5750DW, MFC-L6800DW(T), MFC-L6900DW(T), MFC-L8650CDW, MFC-L8690CDW, MFC-L8850CDW, MFC-L8900CDW, MFC-L9550CDW(T), MFC-L9570CDW(T)

Figure 126 Abundance of compatible printers with admin tool

CASE STUDY: Riding the Printer Pwnie

Send a remote PRN file to any Brother printer with no authentication

A PRN file is a printer driver file. In 2000 & 2006 HP had egg on their face when printer driver files on their website were infected. When the virus was installed: " attempts to reboot the PC. On Windows NT machines, it attempts to change system settings" Although not the same type of attack as back in the day. You can do lots of naughty things with drivers. Windows 64 systems require signed drivers. However, there are ways to circumvent this. I love PowerShell, for offensive purposes. There are PowerShell scripts that can help bypass this requirement.

Figure 127 Think of all the evil things you can do

No login, just attach with the admin tool, then you can send a PRN format file. This should apply to any of the compatible printers. After testing a file on my printer, it went haywire, then shut down. It took numerous power cycles and a full reset of the printer to get it back. I was sweating to fix it before my partner got home. I'm not allowed to hack hardware in the house anymore, not even the Roomba :-(

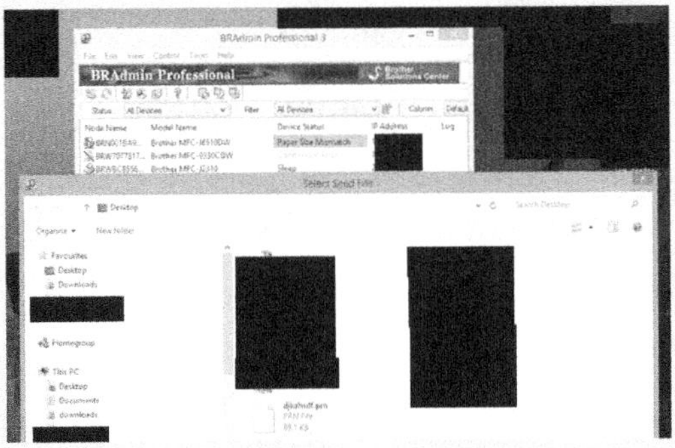

ZAP path transversal

Once you have an IP address, and you're allowed to test the printer. You can use OWASP's ZAP tool and scan the printer's web services. A basic scan revealed a login URL path transversal vulnerability. So much can be found with ZAP, too much for one post. A Dork can also be crafted and used to detect the printers on the internet. Using parameters looking for "/general/status.html" in the URL, then refined or with additional parameters.

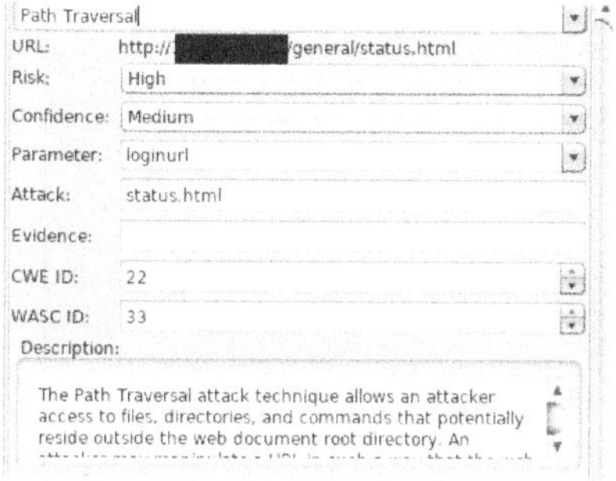

Figure 129 Parameter = loginurl happy hacker joy joy

XSS and unsanitised field fun

The printer web interfaces don't appear to have been security tested that well. My printer isn't the newest ink guzzler on the block. However, taking into account the other exploitable and vulnerable components; it's doubtful looking at the printer web interfaces were tested at all for security purposes.

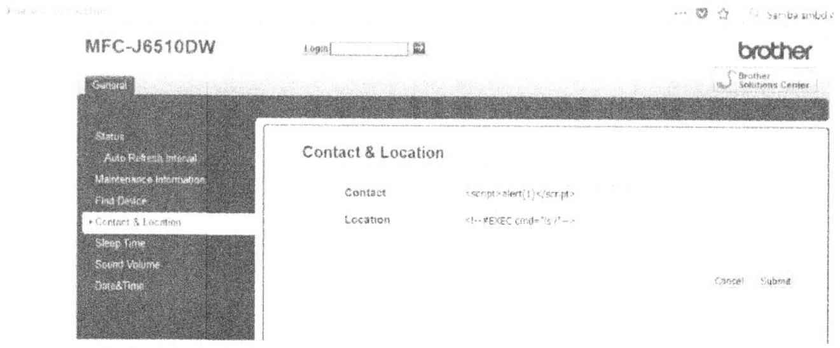

Figure 130 Input

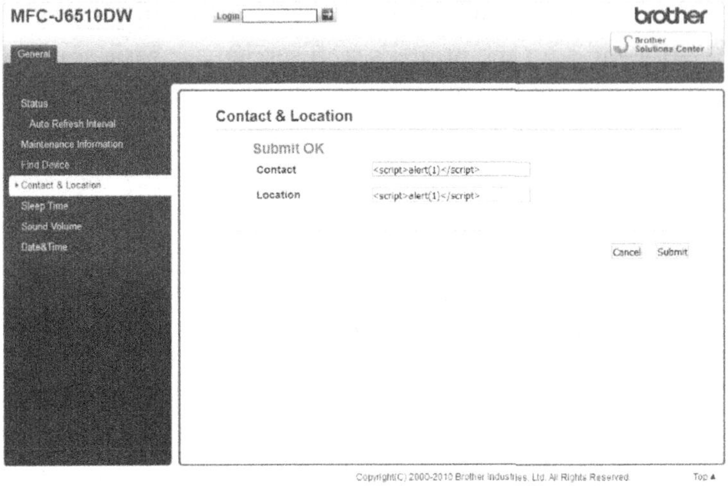

Figure 131 Accepts field submission

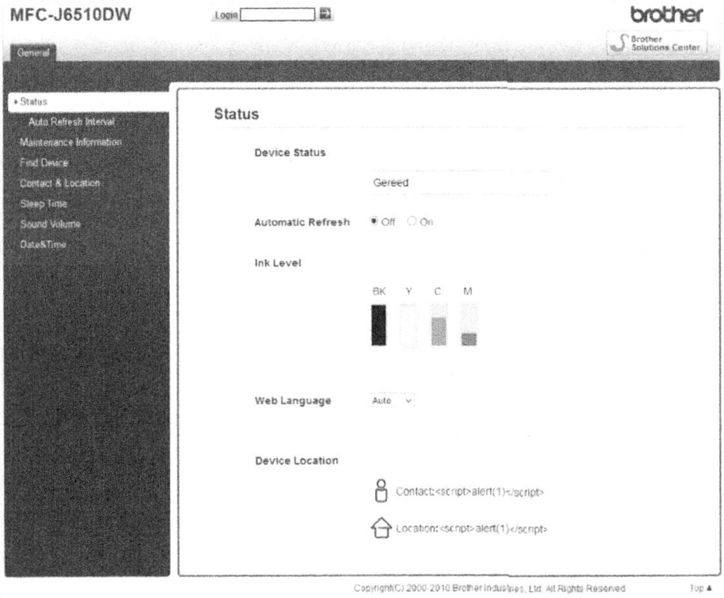

Figure 132 You can call me Mr. <script>alert(1)</script> ;-)

CASE STUDY: Riding the Printer Pwnie

Remote File Inclusion

The login field in the Brother form on several web pages isn't adequately sanitised or filtered against dangerous user input. By modifying the field, external web pages, and files; as well as, other malicious activity can be carried out. This vulnerability also bypasses any login permissions. Post replay with modification of form element because it accepts a URL. I could probably have it open up naughty files and other things. I used both ZAP and Fiddler 4 as a proxy to test and prove. The user agent string doesn't matter.

Vulnerable request(1.2.3.4 fake IP)

POST http://1.2.3.4/general/status.html HTTP/1.1

Host: 1.2.3.4

Referer: http://1.2.3.4/general/contact.html

Content-Type: **application/x-www-form-urlencoded**

Ncb=ZAP&loginurl=https%3A%2F%2Fwww.reddit.com

What you receive back is <title>Reddit</> or Google or whatever you want to partially open via the printer web interface.

```
<!doctype html><html itemscope="" itemtype="http://schema.org/WebPage" lang="nl"><head><m
"/images/branding/googleg/1x/googleg_standard_color_128dp.png" itemprop="image"><link hre
"shortcut icon"><meta content="origin" id="mref" name="referrer"><title>Google</title>
'oYUdWrWYCIHewAKyjLKgBw',kEXPI:
'18168,201794,1354276,1354442,1354723,1354915,1355609,1355736,1355793,1355923,1356033,135
8214,4038394,4041776,4043492,4045096,4045293,4045841,4047140,4047454,4048347,4048980,4050
724,4064468,4064796,4069829,4076999,4078430,4078588,4080760,4081039,4081164,4082230,40892
16,4102237,4103473,4103845,4103861,4104202,4104258,4106647,4108512,4109293,4109316,410949
1,4116926,4116935,4117328,4117980,4118226,4118798,4120420,4120661,4120911,4121035,4121518
,4127744,4127863,4128586,4128624,4129001,4129520,4129556,4129633,4130560,4130776,4130782,
4132956,4133090,4133113,4133416,4134270,4134919,4134948,4135088,4135576,4135744,4135854,4
```

Figure 133 Yummy

Conclusion

Figure 134 Hope one of these isn't exposing something important, like a hospital network.....

Utilising printers as attack tools isn't theoretical and makes for an interesting and potentially juicy target. Printers are connected to your network, they have information about your network, sometimes in-built administrative tools which can be dual used and can be used as a stealthier attack pivot to get deeper into a network. Printers and multi-function scanners are usually over looked for security testing, patching, risk assessment or included in security policies. There is no printer anti-virus, or next-generation printer intrusion protection systems and typically have limited to no usable logs for security purposes. There is a reason Censys.io has written the ability to tag detected printer devices.

Back in 2017, I began trying to report these issues to Brother to no avail. Sadly, Brother didn't respond, and there's no bug bounty program. Off to a CERT as a vulnerability report. Printers aren't super sexy, but they can provide a lovely pivot point for attackers with imagination. An attacker only needs to get lucky once. You have to be lucky every time. Don't make it easy, secure your printer with a password, limit exposure to the outside world. Please, for the love of God, don't trust that scheming plastic ink killer.

References

9 Vladimir Putin quotes that offer terrifying insights into his mind – Business Insider
https://www.businessinsider.com/hard-core-putin-quotes-2017-6/?international=true&r=US&IR=T

Riding the Printer Pwnie – Chris Kubecka
https://hackernoon.com/riding-the-printer-pwnie-fa9f4ce822ed?source=rss-8218a403853f------2&gi=aa0441d9ecbb

Chapter 11

Reporting

INFORMATION IN THIS CHAPTER:

- Why Censys reporting is useful
- Setting up reports
- Running reports

Although our intellect always longs for clarity and certainty, our nature often finds uncertainty fascinating.

- Carl von Clausewitz

11 Censys Reports

11.1 Censys Reporting

Many of the previous chapters included using the reporting function. This chapter should give you some additional, useful report options and use cases.

11.2 Find Vulnerable IIS servers in an unconventional way

An important part of network security defence is discovering vulnerabilities or other problems before someone with bad intentions does. IIS as a web server has been around for many years; as such, there will be old, vulnerable versions with Metasploit modules and other methods of exploitation.

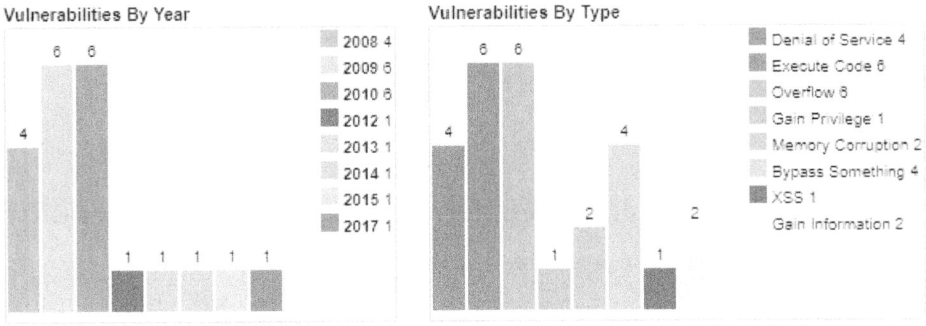

Figure 135 CVE Details.com Microsoft IIS Vulnerabilities

There have been security tools like IIS Lockdown, security advisories and Troy Hunt equating disclosing the server in the response headers to PIN theft by ATM skimmer. Unbeknownst to some administrators, the HTTP response headers can be customized IIS using the <customHeaders> in the configuration. ZMap and Censys can banner grab the properties of the headers.

80.http.get.headers.server

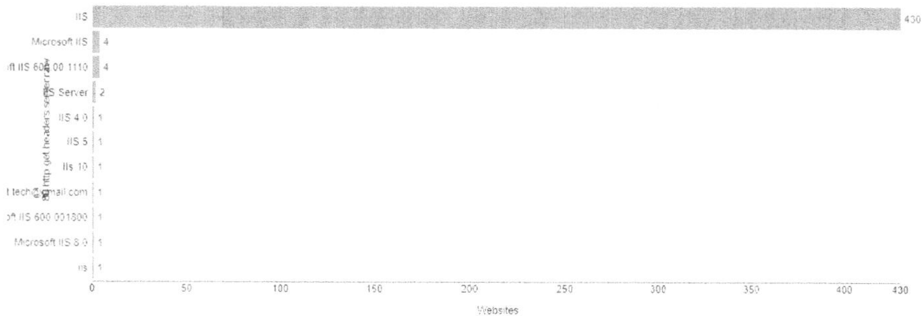

Figure 136 Censys Report Top Ten 80.http.get.headers.server graph

Table 63 Censys Report Top Ten 80.http.get.headers.server

Protocol	Number	Percentage
IIS	430	96.2%
Microsoft IIS	4	0.89%
Microsoft IIS 600.00 1110	4	0.89%
IIS Server	2	0.45%
IIS 4.0	1	0.22%
IIS 5	1	0.22%
IIs 10	1	0.22%
Microsoft IIS 6.0 - Setup and config by duocnt.tech@gmail.com	1	0.22%
Microsoft IIS 600.001800	1	0.22%
Microsoft IIS 8.0	1	0.22%
iis	1	0.22%
Total	447	100%

Click **Microsoft IIS 6.0 - Setup and config by duocnt.tech@gmail.com** or use the search string directly **(80.http.get.headers.server: IIS) AND 80.http.get.headers.server: "Microsoft IIS 6.0 - Setup and config by duocnt.tech@gmail.com"**

Figure 137 Censys report result for email in IIS banner

11.3 SMTP Ciphers

25.smtp.starttls.tls.cipher_suite by name

Find the worldwide names, frequency, number of hosts **https://censys.io/ipv4/report?q=&field=25.smtp.starttls.tls.cipher_suite.name.raw&max_buckets=**

Drill down and focus on country of **China**
Then focus on the details of the first listed host. A common theme will be Chinese modems.

Figure 138 Chinese vulnerable modems

11.4 Build a report for the Top 10 Modbus Web Servers

If you remember in the ICS & SCADA chapter, the Modbus ius a fragile protocol which requires no authentication and will accept a command from any device if encoded properly. Well, many of these devices have web servers too. The report can be long, but we want to restrict it to **10 buckets maximum**. In the web search use the string, the click **Reports** and use **80.http.get.headers.server**.

protocols.raw: "502/modbus"

or the direct search string

https://censys.io/ipv4/report?q=protocols.raw%3A+%22502%2Fmodbus%22&field=80.http.get.headers.server.raw&max_buckets=10

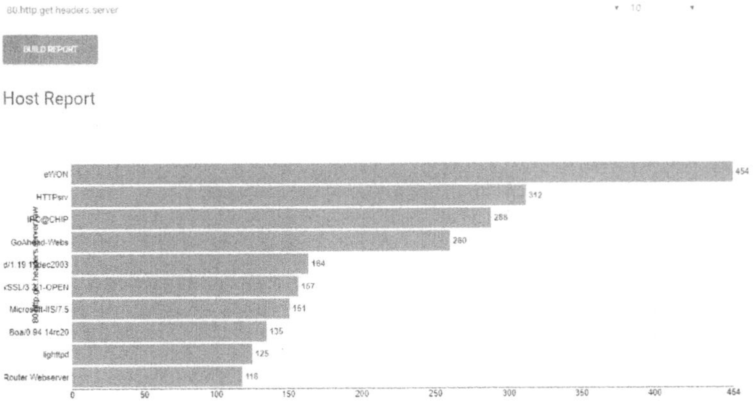

Figure 139 Censys Top 10 web servers graph on Modbus devices

Table 64 Censys Top 10 web server Host Report on Modbus devices

Banner	Number	Percentage
eWON	454	6.67%
HTTPsrv	312	4.59%
IPC@CHIP	288	4.23%
GoAhead-Webs	260	3.82%
mini_httpd/1.19 19dec2003	164	2.41%
Goahead/2.5.0 PeerSec-MatrixSSL/3.2.1-OPEN	157	2.31%
Microsoft-IIS/7.5	151	2.22%
Boa/0.94.14rc20	135	1.98%
lighttpd	125	1.84%
Router Webserver	118	1.73%

Other	4,640	68.2%

Go to **cvedetails.com** and type **IIS 7.5** in the search bar.

Microsoft » IIS » 7.5 : **Security Vulnerabilities**

Cpe Name:*cpe:/a:microsoft:iis:7.5*
CVSS Scores Greater Than: 0 1 2 3 4 5 6 7 8 9
Sort Results By : CVE Number Descending CVE Number Ascending CVSS Score Descending Number Of Exploits Descending
Copy Results Download Results

#	CVE ID	CWE ID	# of Exploits	Vulnerability Type(s)	Publish Date	Update Date	Score
1	CVE-2012-2531	200		+Info	2012-11-13	2017-09-18	2.1
Microsoft Internet Information Services (IIS) 7.5 uses weak permissions for the Operational log, which allows local user							
2	CVE-2010-3972	119	1	DoS Exec Code Overflow +Info	2010-12-23	2017-09-18	10.0
Heap-based buffer overflow in the TELNET_STREAM_CONTEXT::OnSendData function in ftpsvc.dll in Microsoft FTP Servi execute arbitrary code or cause a denial of service (daemon crash) via a crafted FTP command, aka "IIS FTP Service He information.							
3	CVE-2010-2730	119		Exec Code Overflow	2010-09-15	2017-09-18	9.3
Buffer overflow in Microsoft Internet Information Services (IIS) 7.5, when FastCGI is enabled, allows remote attackers t Vulnerability."							
4	CVE-2010-1899	119		DoS Overflow	2010-09-15	2017-09-18	4.3
Stack consumption vulnerability in the ASP implementation in Microsoft Internet Information Services (IIS) 5.1, 6.0, 7.0 request, related to asp.dll, aka "IIS Repeated Parameter Request Denial of Service Vulnerability."							
5	CVE-2010-1256	94		Exec Code Mem. Corr.	2010-06-08	2017-09-18	8.5
Unspecified vulnerability in Microsoft IIS 6.0, 7.0, and 7.5, when Extended Protection for Authentication is enabled, allo							

Figure 140 CVEDetails listing IIS 7.5 vulnerabilities

11.5 Discovering vulnerable SSH servers

Let's explore the table below the graph. It shows the banner of the SSH scanned. SSH, like most things, has vulnerable versions. The version 1.99 banner is the way a server tells perspective clients it supports both SSHv1 and SSHv2. SSH version 1.5 however, is vulnerable due to poor integrity checking, can be exploited exposing the session keys which can allow decryption and injection of data into encrypted packets. The vulnerabilities in version 1.5 have been well known since 2001.

Using the search string

protocols.raw: "22/ssh"

then click Report, then select from the drop down

22.ssh.v2.banner.version

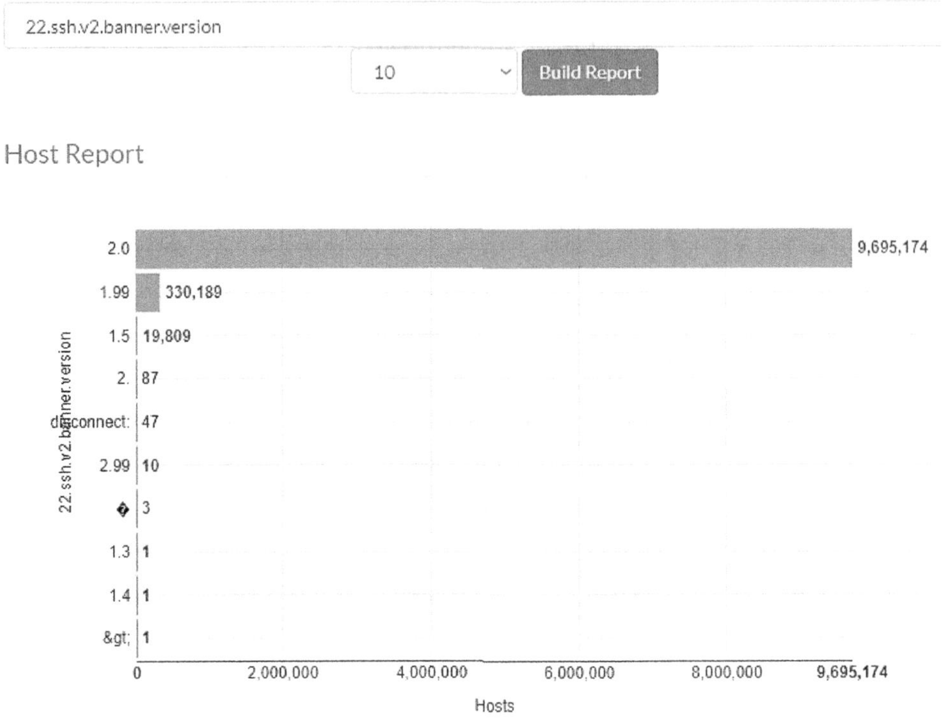

Figure 141 Censys Top Ten report 22.ssh.v2.banner.version

Table 65 Censys Top 10 report 22.ssh.v2.banner.version

Banner	Number	Percentage
2.0	9,695,174	96.51%
1.99	330.189	3.29%
1.5	19,809	0.2%
2.	87	0.0%
disconnect	47	0.0%
2.99	10	0.0%

?	3	0.0%
1.3	1	0.0%
1.4	1	0.0%
Other	4	0.0%
Total	10,045,325	100%

Next, we are looking for vulnerable systems and exploits. Version 1.5 is vulnerable to exploit. How easy is it to exploit SSH version 1.5? For point and click testing, there are Metasploit modules available. Meaning, somewhat easy.

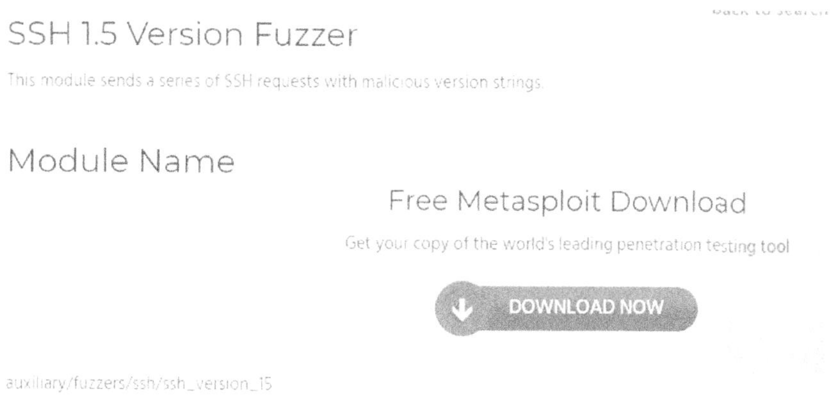

Figure 142 Metasploit SSH version 1.5 exploit module

https://www.rapid7.com/db/modules/auxiliary/fuzzers/ssh/ssh_version_15

11.6 What is running in Iran
location.country: iran

Select **Tools, Query Metadata**

Country Breakdown

Country	Hosts	Frequency
Iran	329,275	100.0%

Figure 143 Iranian Country Metadata

Network Breakdown

Autonomous System (AS)	Hosts	Frequency
DCI-AS, IR	57,110	17.34%
RASANA, IR	29,814	9.05%
TCI, IR	20,130	6.11%
PARSONLINE Tehran - IRAN, IR	19,338	5.87%
TIC-AS, IR	15,382	4.67%
RESPINA-AS, IR	13,311	4.04%
MEGASERVERS-FFM, DE	9,076	2.76%
ASIATECH, IR	8,624	2.62%
IR-THR-PTE, IR	7,955	2.42%
NGSAS, IR	6,578	2.0%

Figure 144 Major networks in Iran

Common Tags

Tag	Hosts	Frequency
http	209,852	63.73%
embedded	77,255	23.46%
dns	59,651	18.12%
network	49,123	14.92%
https	48,126	14.62%
ftp	44,051	13.38%
telnet	33,179	10.08%
ssh	30,717	9.33%
smtp	24,642	7.48%
smb	23,180	7.04%

Figure 145 Censys Iran metadata report Common Tags

11.7 North Korea has the internet?

https://www.northkoreatech.org/2011/06/26/north-koreas-chinese-ip-addresses/

Yes, the Democratic People's Republic of Korea has the internet. They also have their own flavor of Linux called Red Star. There are at least two well-known IP ranges associated with North Korea. However, these can changer. The main associated IP range is 175.45.178.0/24. A well-known network owned by North Korea is Star KP Ryugyong-dong. KP us the country code for North Korea.

Open the web version of Censys, login and enter as the search term: **location.country: "north korea"** and search all criteria. Almost 130 hosts returned in milliseconds.

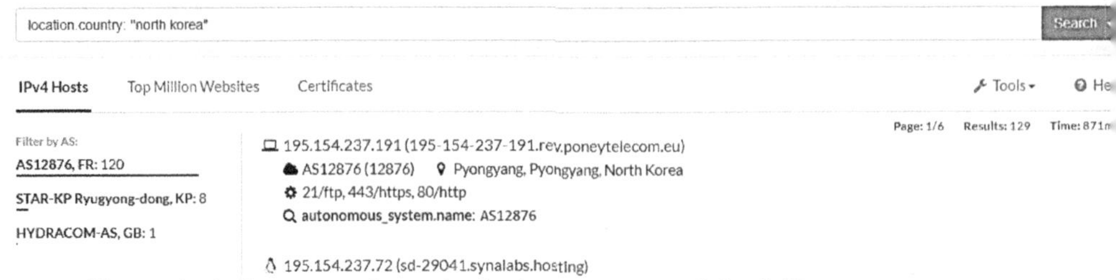

Figure 146 Censys search results for location.country North Korea

Let's sort the data differently and go to **Tools**, then **Query Metadata**. Although all the returned hosts say they are located in North Korea, it doesn't necessarily mean they are physically located in North Korea. Focusing on a known North Korea provider, Star.

Network Breakdown

Autonomous System (AS)	Hosts	Frequency
AS12876, FR	120	93.02%
STAR-KP Ryugyong-dong, KP	8	6.2%
HYDRACOM-AS, GB	1	0.78%

Figure 147 Censys Metadata report North Korea Network Breakdown

Filtering further, you can click the hyperlinked STAR-KP Ryugyong-dong KP or search using **(location.country: "north korea") AND autonomous_system.description.raw: "STAR-KP Ryugyong-dong, KP"**

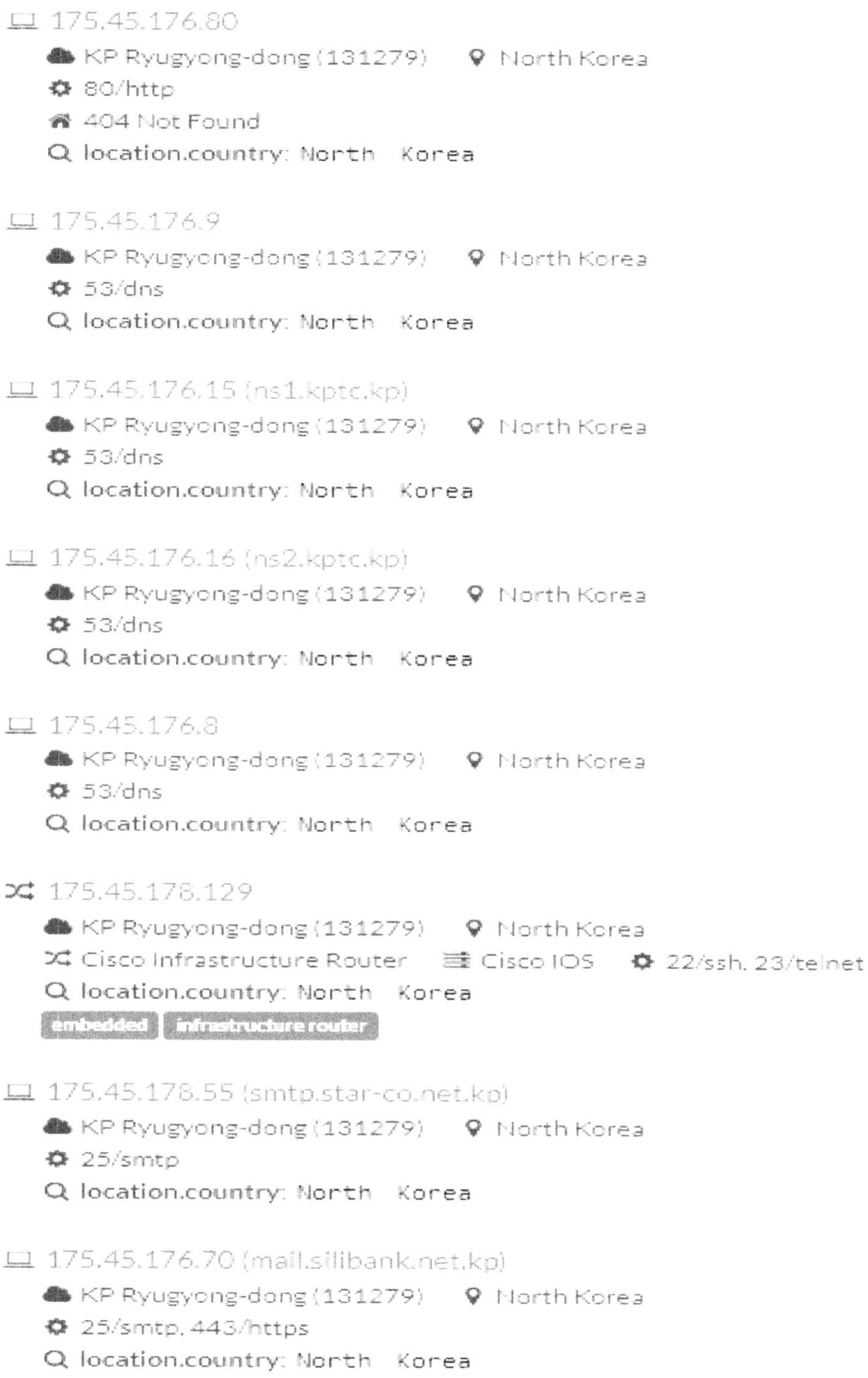

Figure 148 Censys STAR Ryugyong-dong KP network DPRK search

results

Looking into the details of Silibank:

Figure 149 Censys mail.silibank.net.kp details

Figure 150 Censys mail.silibank.net.kp Whois details

11.8 Discovering SMTP Start TLS Configurations

There are two main methods of getting the Start TLS configuration settings from Censys.io via the web search.

Use the direct search string:

https://censys.io/ipv4/report?q=25.smtp.starttls.starttls&field=25.smtp.starttls.starttls.raw&max_buckets=

Or, use in the web search

25.smtp.starttls.starttls

Then select Report, by the field **25.smtp.starttls.starttls.raw** and **50** Buckets

Table 66 Censys SMTP Start TLS Configuration

Tag	Hosts	Frequency
220 2.0.0 Ready to start TLS	1,627,987	26.8%
220 TLS go ahead	865,984	14.26%
502 5.5.1 Error: command not implemented	733,231	12.07%
502 5.5.1 command not supported in "STARTTLS"	451,026	7.42%
454 4.3.3 TLS not available after start	297,997	4.91%
220 2.0.0 SMTP server ready	259,837	4.28%
502 unimplemented (#5.5.1)	257,214	4.23%
220 Ready to start TLS	213,560	3.52%
220 ready for tls	196,631	3.24%
220 Begin TLS negotiation	172,735	2.84%
503 Bad sequence of commands	153,572	2.53%
502 5.5.2 Error: command not recognized	72,931	1.2%
554 5.7.3 Unable to initialize security subsystem	71,376	1.17%
220 2.0.0 Start TLS	63,256	1.04%
454 TLS not available due to temporary reason	44,510	0.73%
503 STARTTLS command used	43,779	0.72%

when not advertised		
500 Unrecognized command	38,969	0.64%
220 Go ahead with TLS	28,171	0.46%
502 No such command	27,115	0.45%
503 TLS is not allowed	26,930	0.44%
454 TLS not available	25,286	0.42%
500 Syntax error, command unrecognized	22,844	0.38%
500 5.5.1 command unknown in "STARTTLS"	18,334	0.3%
220 2.0.0 ready to start TLS	17,347	0.29%
220 Proceed.	15,762	0.26%
502 Unimplemented command.	15,272	0.25%
454 4.7.0 TLS not available due to local problem	13,856	0.23%
500 5.5.2 unrecognized command	13,473	0.22%
502 unimplemented	13,115	0.22%
402 4.5.1 Error: command not implemented	12,589	0.21%
454 TLS currently unavailable	11,582	0.19%
502 Error: command not implemented	10,865	0.18%
502 Command not implemented	10,779	0.18%

220 2.7.0 Ready to start TLS	10,320	0.17%
500 #5.5.1 command not recognized	10,156	0.17%
454 TLS missing certificate: error:02001002:system library:fopen:No such file or directory (#4.3.0)	9,884	0.16%
500 5.5.1 Command unrecognized: "STARTTLS"	9,106	0.15%
500 Command unrecognized	8,915	0.15%
500 server disabled STARTTLS	8,274	0.14%
220 Start TLS negotiation	7,140	0.12%
500 5.0.0 'STARTTLS': command not understood.	6,739	0.11%
220 2.0.0 continue	4,849	0.08%
220 ready for TLS/SSL	4,780	0.08%
220 Go ahead	4,764	0.08%
454 4.7.0 TLS not available	4,411	0.07%
502 STARTTLS NOT ALLOWED.	3,768	0.06%
454 4.4.3 TLS not available: not configured	3,482	0.06%
220 please start a TLS connection	3,426	0.06%
500 unrecognized command	3,141	0.05%
220 2.2.0 Ready to start TLS	3,029	0.05%

Other	120,754	1.99%
Total	6,074,853	100.0%

11.9 Discovering SMTP servers with Command implementation errors

We are looking for SMTP email servers with errors. If there are errors, likely there are other issues. Use the search string, IPv4:

25.smtp.starttls.starttls: "502 5.5.1 Error: command not implemented"

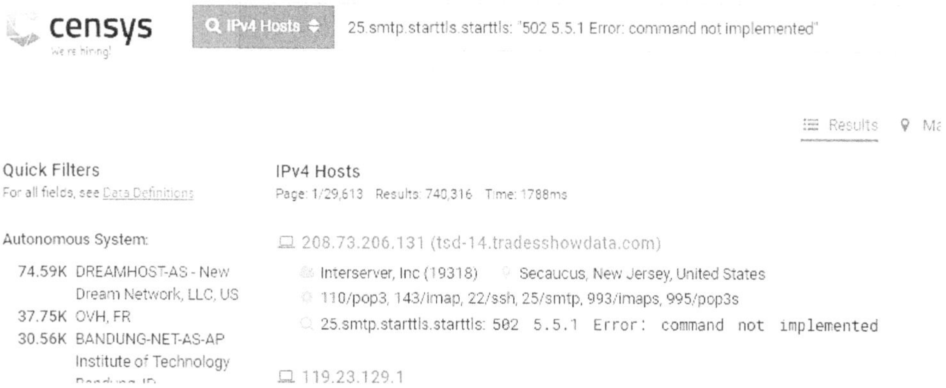

Figure 151 Censys SMTP Start TLS code 502 5.5.1 error code

Next, build a report to show the manufacturers. Press the Report link, then select **Metadata.manufacturer and 10 buckets**

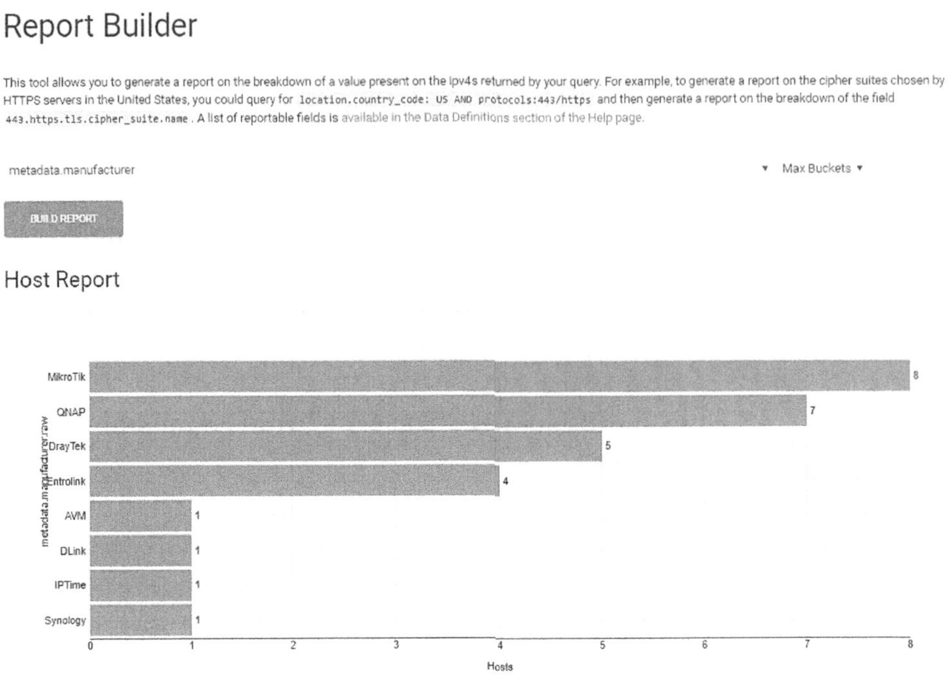

Figure 152 Censys SMTP Start TLS code 552 5.5.1 Metadata.manufacturer.raw graph

Table 67 Censys SMTP Start TLS code 552 5.5.1 Metadata.manufacturer.raw report

Tag	Hosts	Frequency
MikroTik	8	28.57%
QNAP	7	25.0%
DrayTek	5	17.86%
Entrolink	4	14.29%
AVM	1	3.57%
DLink	1	3.57%
IPTime	1	3.57%

Synology	1	3.57%
Total	28	100.0%

25.smtp.starttls.starttls: "502 5.5.1 Error: command not implemented" AND tags: database

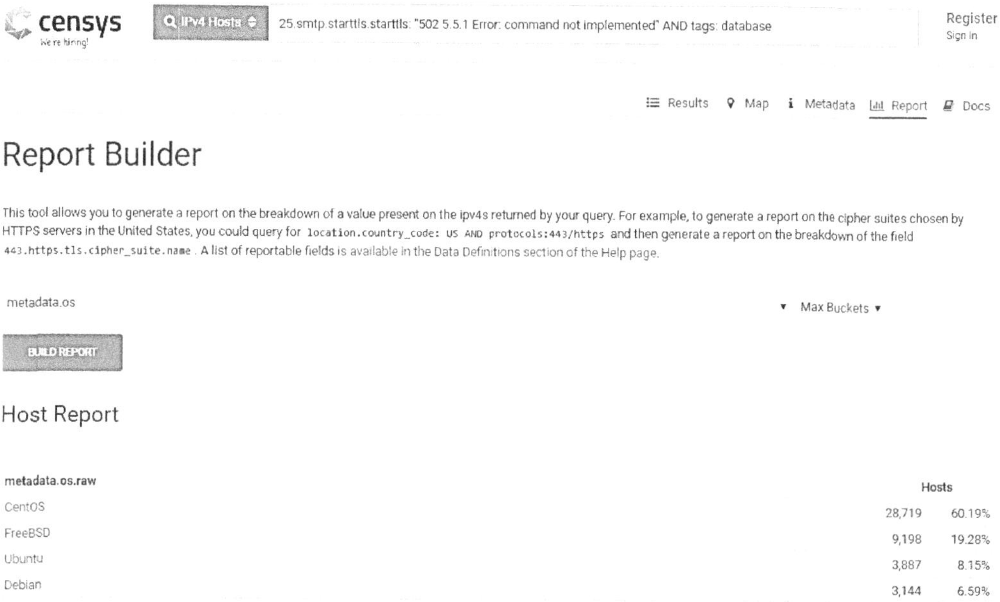

https://censys.io/ipv4/report?q=25.smtp.starttls.starttls%3A+%22502+5.5.1+Error%3A+command+not+implemented%22+AND+tags%3A+database&field=metadata.os.raw&max_buckets=

Metadata.os.raw	Hosts	Frequency
CentOS	28,719	60.19%
FreeBSD	9,198	19.28%
Ubuntu	3,887	8.15%

Debian	3,144	6.59%
Unix	930	1.95%
RedHat	725	1.52%
Fedora	370	0.78%
Amazon	212	0.44%
Turbolinux	167	0.35%
Windows	160	0.34%
EL	68	0.14%
FH	31	0.06%
IUS	19	0.04%
Win32	13	0.03%
Oracle	12	0.03%
PowerStack	9	0.02%
MikroTik RouterOS	6	0.01%
Raspbian	5	0.01%
Sangoma	5	0.01%
cPanel	5	0.01%
Linux	4	0.01%
NetBSD	4	0.01%
Win64	4	0.01%
codeit	3	0.01%

Novell	2	0.0%
Perl	2	0.0%
Unixadm.org	2	0.0%
1.el6_10.wing	1	0.0%
ASPLinux	1	0.0%
CentOS64	1	0.0%
ClearOS	1	0.0%
Gentoo	1	0.0%
SuSE	1	0.0%
SuliX	1	0.0%
UNIX	1	0.0%
centos	1	0.0%
Total	47,715	100.0%

Other useful SMTP queries and reports

https://censys.io/ipv4/report?q=25.smtp.starttls.starttls&field=25.smtp.starttls.starttls.raw&max_buckets=

```
"query": "25.smtp.starttls.starttls"
```

(25.smtp.starttls.starttls) AND 25.smtp.starttls.starttls: "502 5.5.1 Error: command not implemented421 4.7.0 deploy.by.yhsrv.com Error: too many errors"
https://censys.io/ipv4?q=%2825.smtp.starttls.starttls%29+AND+25.smtp.starttls.starttls%3A+"502+5.5.1+Error%3A+command+not+implemented%0D%0A421+4.7.0+deploy.by.yhsrv.com+Error%3A+too+many+errors"&collection=

(25.smtp.starttls.starttls) AND 25.smtp.starttls.starttls: "error"

25.smtp.starttls.starttls
454 TLS not available due to temporary reason
454 4.3.3 TLS not available after start

25.smtp.starttls.ehlo
250-**barracuda.ord1**.reflected.net Hello
CLIENT_HOSTNAME [CLIENT_IP], pleased to meet you
250-SIZE 100000000
250-PIPELINING
250-8BITMIME
250 HELP

0.lookup.spf.raw
v=spf1 mx:mail.pornhub.com ptr:closedrelay.com
ip4:94.199.255.10/32 ip4:208.91.206.64/26
ip4:66.254.113.78/32 ptr:reflected.net ip4:66.254.119.174
ip4:66.254.113.78 ip4:66.254.112.72/30 -all

0.lookup.axfr.servers
{u'status': u'ERROR', u'server': u'204.13.250.44', u'error': u'dns: bad xfr rcode: 5'}, {u'status': u'ERROR', u'server': u'208.78.71.44', u'error': u'dial tcp 208.78.71.44:53: i/o timeout'}, {u'status': u'ERROR', u'server': u'156.154.143.3', u'error': u'dns: bad xfr rcode: 5'}, {u'status': u'ERROR', u'server': u'156.154.141.3', u'error': u'dns: bad xfr rcode: 5'}, {u'status': u'ERROR', u'server': u'208.78.70.44', u'error': u'dns: bad xfr rcode: 5'}, {u'status': u'ERROR', u'server': u'156.154.142
0.lookup.axfr.support
False
0.lookup.axfr.truncated
False

110.pop3.starttls.banner
+OK bhpstrefa.home.pl IdeaPop3Server 0.82 ready.
110.pop3.starttls.starttls
+OK Begin TLS negotiation

The SMTP protocol has numerous error codes which can help diagnose and discover problematic systems.

11.10 Discovering DNS Open Resolvers

DNS Open resolvers are insecurely configured DNS servers which attackers can use in various types of attacks. There's a nifty tool which can check any hosts Censys finds: **http://www.openresolver.com/**

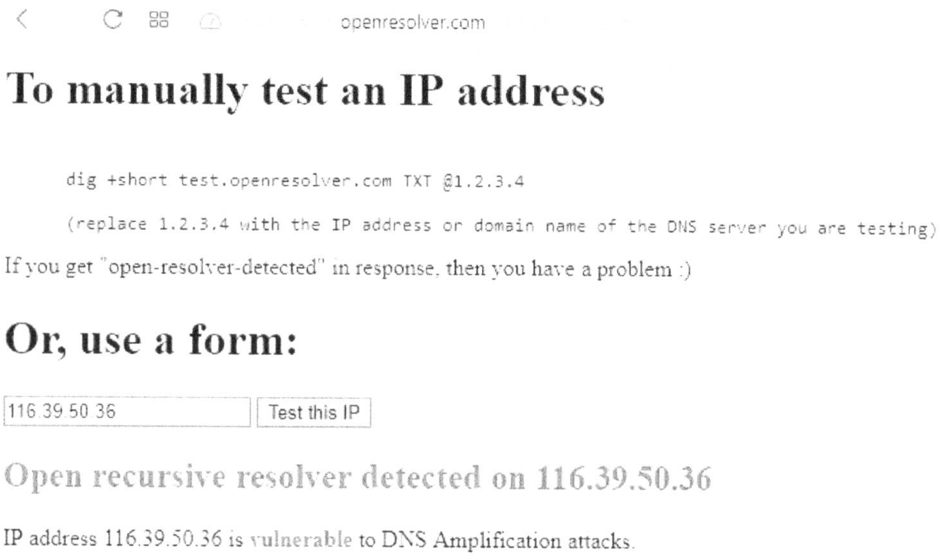

https://www.us-cert.gov/ncas/alerts/TA13-088A

To find these systems on Censys, run a Report using:

53.dns.open_resolver

Figure 153 Censys DNS Open Resolver is False

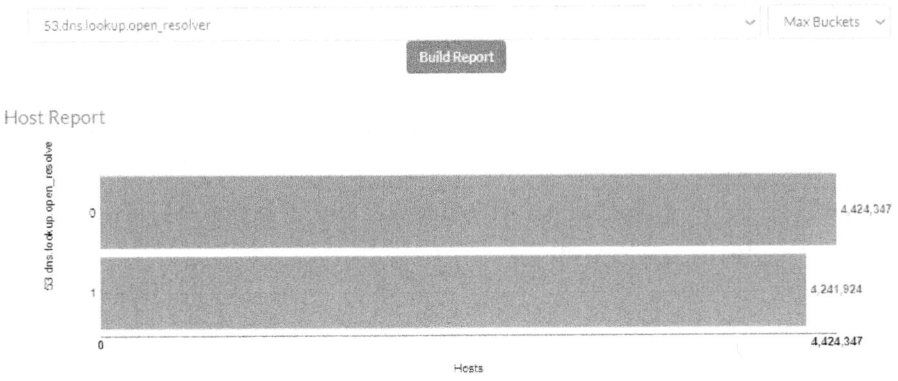

Raw Data

53.dns.lookup.open_resolver	Hosts	
0	4,424,347	51.05%
1	4,241,924	48.95%
Total	8,666,271	100.0%

Figure 154 Censys report DNS open resolvers vs.. non November 2017

IPv4 Hosts · Top Million Websites · Certificates · Tools · Help

Your query (`53.dns.lookup.open_resolver: "0"`) found 4,589,313 IPv4 hosts.

Country Breakdown

Country	Hosts	Frequency
United States	1,698,881	37.02%
China	504,916	11.0%
Germany	238,792	5.2%
France	176,671	3.85%
United Kingdom	172,267	3.75%
Russia	163,257	3.56%
Turkey	127,811	2.78%
Netherlands	125,536	2.74%
Canada	100,790	2.2%
Japan	88,047	1.92%

Network Breakdown

Autonomous System (AS)	Hosts	Frequency
CTTNET China TieTong Telecommunications Corporation, CN	328,564	7.16%
OVH, FR	285,521	6.22%
INCAPSULA - Incapsula Inc, US	91,206	1.99%
LIQUIDWEB - Liquid Web, L.L.C, US	89,950	1.96%
UNIFIEDLAYER-AS-1 - Unified Layer, US	86,166	1.88%
CNNIC-HCENET-AP HEXIE Information technology Co., Ltd., CN	82,085	1.79%
HETZNER-AS, DE	75,838	1.65%
SINGLEHOP-LLC - SingleHop, Inc., US	67,767	1.48%
CYRUSONE - CyrusOne LLC, US	63,966	1.39%
AS-26496-GO-DADDY-COM-LLC - GoDaddy.com, LLC, US	58,188	1.27%

Common Tags

Tag	Hosts	Frequency
dns	4,589,313	100.0%
http	3,212,759	70.01%
pop3	2,276,667	49.61%
ftp	2,249,384	49.01%
imap	2,222,540	48.43%
imaps	2,194,004	47.81%
pop3s	2,147,399	46.79%
https	1,937,202	42.21%
smtp	1,451,333	31.62%
ssh	1,394,166	30.38%

Figure 155 DNS Open Resolver Metadata

53.dns.lookup.open_resolver Max Buckets Build Report

Host Report

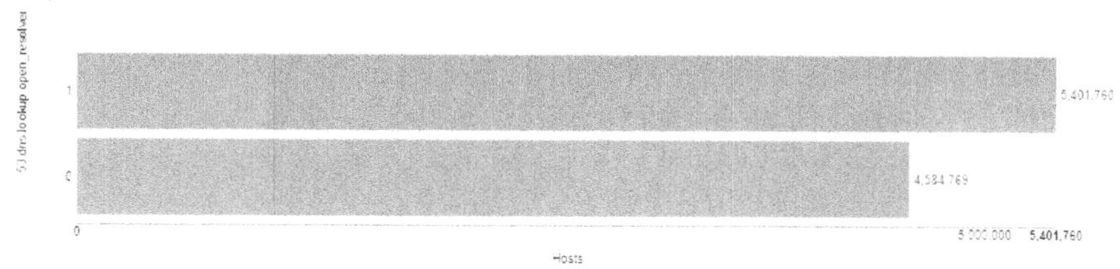

Raw Data

53.dns.lookup.open_resolver	Hosts	
1	5,401,760	54.09%
0	4,584,769	45.91%
Total	9,986,529	100.0%

Figure 156 Censys report DNS open resolvers vs.. non March 2018

IPv4 Hosts Top Million Websites Certificates Tools Help

Your query (`53.dns.lookup.open_resolver: "1"`) found 5,437,227 IPv4 hosts.

Country Breakdown

Country	Hosts	Frequency
China	2,187,780	40.24%
United States	486,245	8.94%
Brazil	249,419	4.59%
Taiwan	241,321	4.44%
Republic of Korea	211,563	3.89%
Russia	202,574	3.73%
India	195,431	3.59%
Italy	103,944	1.91%
Turkey	103,666	1.91%
Canada	99,272	1.83%

Network Breakdown

Autonomous System (AS)	Hosts	Frequency
CHINANET-BACKBONE No.31,Jin-rong Street, CN	1,228,862	22.6%
CHINA169-BACKBONE CHINA UNICOM China169 Backbone, CN	521,005	9.58%
HINET Data Communication Business Group, TW	220,661	4.06%
KIXS-AS-KR Korea Telecom, KR	176,143	3.24%
CHINANET-SH-AP China Telecom (Group), CN	110,837	2.04%
CNIX-AP China Networks Inter-Exchange, CN	109,409	2.01%
BSNL-NIB National Internet Backbone, IN	99,455	1.83%
ROSTELECOM-AS, RU	78,722	1.45%
TELEFNICA BRASIL S.A, BR	75,321	1.39%
ASN-IBSNAZ, IT	72,294	1.33%

Common Tags

Tag	Hosts	Frequency
dns	5,437,227	100.0%
http	1,042,009	19.16%
ftp	533,304	9.81%
https	397,774	7.32%
ssh	329,407	6.06%
embedded	305,920	5.63%
telnet	305,534	5.62%
pop3	231,656	4.26%
imap	210,054	3.86%
smtp	159,151	2.93%

53.dns.lookup.errors	True
53.dns.lookup.open_resolver	False
53.dns.lookup.questions	{u'type': u'A', u'name': u'c.afekv.com'}
53.dns.lookup.resolves_correctly	False
53.dns.lookup.support	True
autonomous_system.asn	665
autonomous_system.country_code	US
autonomous_system.description	DNIC-ASBLK-00616-00665 - DoD Network Information Center, US
autonomous_system.name	DNIC-ASBLK-00616-00665
autonomous_system.organization	DoD Network Information Center

Figure 157 Censys DNS Lookup Errors on a DOD DNS server

To discover DNS servers which are not Open Resolvers:

(53.dns.open_resolver.metadata) AND 53.dns.lookup.errors: "1"

Autonomous Systems (AS)	Hosts	Frequency
OVH, FR	334,588	5.17%
HOMEPL-AS, PL	169,598	2.62%
ERX-TANET-ASN1 Taiwan Academic Network (TANet) Information Center, TW	154,191	2.38%
CPI-NET KDDI Web Communications Inc., JP	138,520	2.14%
HETZNER-AS, DE	129,239	2.0%
INFOSPHERE NTT PC Communications, Inc., JP	114,590	1.77%
OCN NTT Communications Corporation, JP	87,739	1.36%
DIGITALOCEAN-ASN - DigitalOcean, LLC, US	86,986	1.34%

DREAMHOST-AS - New Dream Network, LLC, US	83,615	1.29%
SOLTIA, ES	82,925	1.28%

Autonomous Systems (AS)	Hosts	Frequency
OVH, FR	334,588	5.17%
HOMEPL-AS, PL	169,598	2.62%
ERX-TANET-ASN1 Taiwan Academic Network (TANet) Information Center, TW	154,191	2.38%
CPI-NET KDDI Web Communications Inc., JP	138,520	2.14%
HETZNER-AS, DE	129,239	2.0%
INFOSPHERE NTT PC Communications, Inc., JP	114,590	1.77%
OCN NTT Communications Corporation, JP	87,739	1.36%
DIGITALOCEAN-ASN - DigitalOcean, LLC, US	86,986	1.34%
DREAMHOST-AS - New Dream Network, LLC, US	83,615	1.29%
SOLTIA, ES	82,925	1.28%

Autonomous Systems (AS)	Hosts	Frequency
OVH, FR	334,588	5.17%
HOMEPL-AS, PL	169,598	2.62%
ERX-TANET-ASN1 Taiwan Academic Network (TANet) Information Center, TW	154,191	2.38%
CPI-NET KDDI Web Communications Inc., JP	138,520	2.14%
HETZNER-AS, DE	129,239	2.0%
INFOSPHERE NTT PC Communications, Inc., JP	114,590	1.77%
OCN NTT Communications Corporation, JP	87,739	1.36%
DIGITALOCEAN-ASN - DigitalOcean, LLC, US	86,986	1.34%
DREAMHOST-AS - New Dream Network, LLC, US	83,615	1.29%
SOLTIA, ES	82,925	1.28%

"53.dns.lookup.open_resolver: True"
53.dns.lookup.open_resolver: "1"

https://community.infoblox.com/t5/IPv6-CoE-Blog/Finding-and-Fixing-Open-DNS-Resolvers/ba-p/3405

Your query (`53.dns.lookup.open_resolver: True`) found 5.214.688 IPv4 hosts.

Country Breakdown

Country	Hosts	Frequency
China	2.075.389	39.8%
United States	480.296	9.21%
Brazil	235.158	4.51%
Taiwan	227.079	4.35%
Republic of Korea	208.506	4.0%
Russia	194.665	3.73%
India	186.068	3.57%
Turkey	100.544	1.93%
Italy	100.078	1.92%
Canada	98.451	1.89%

Network Breakdown

Autonomous System (AS)	Hosts	Frequency
CHINANET-BACKBONE No.31.Jin-rong Street, CN	1.152.772	22.11%
CHINA169-BACKBONE CHINA UNICOM China169 Backbone, CN	494.447	9.48%
HINET Data Communication Business Group, TW	206.901	3.97%
KIXS-AS-KR Korea Telecom, KR	173.567	3.33%
CNIX-AP China Networks Inter-Exchange, CN	109.040	2.09%
CHINANET-SH-AP China Telecom (Group), CN	108.134	2.07%
BSNL-NIB National Internet Backbone, IN	93.732	1.8%
ROSTELECOM-AS, RU	74.320	1.43%
TELEFNICA BRASIL S.A, BR	69.613	1.33%
ASN-IBSNAZ, IT	69.170	1.33%

Common Tags

Tag	Hosts	Frequency
dns	5.214.517	100.0%
http	1.022.339	19.6%
ftp	528.150	10.13%
https	387.439	7.43%
ssh	324.468	6.22%
telnet	299.378	5.74%
embedded	295.281	5.66%
pop3	231.490	4.44%
imap	209.956	4.03%
smtp	158.963	3.05%

Biggest at the time DDoS used DNS Open Resolvers, Spamhaus March 2013 300 Gbps

Figure 158 Censys DNS Open Resolver search results

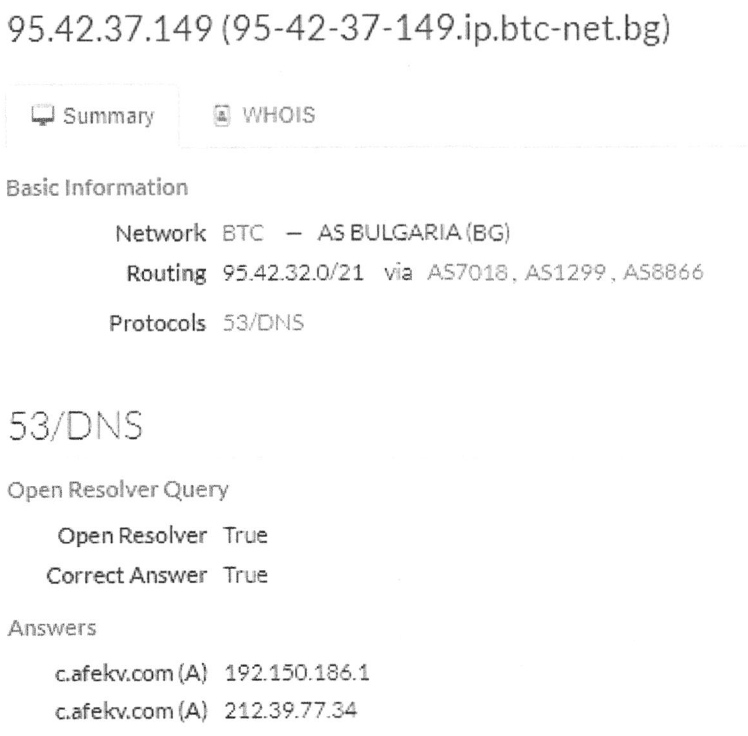

Figure 159 Censys Bulgarian DNS Open Resolver example

One of the reasons why so many attacks seem to come from China. The country has weaker configurations, one reason is due to government mandated backdoors. If we zoom in on Query Metadata in Tools. Over 38% of all the Censys scanned DNS Open Resolvers are located in China. Almost two million weak points which can be aimed and used to attack.

Country Breakdown

Country	Hosts	Frequency
China	1,921,096	38.85%
United States	469,669	9.5%
Brazil	220,568	4.46%
Taiwan	207,010	4.19%
Republic of Korea	202,147	4.09%
Russia	197,189	3.99%
India	177,646	3.59%
Canada	96,977	1.96%
Turkey	96,460	1.95%
Italy	95,801	1.94%

Figure 160 Censys DNS Open Resolver Country Breakdown

11.11 Discovering vulnerable Telnet service banners and settings

Search string in the web

protocols.raw: "23/telnet"

Then click **Report**, then select from the drop down

23.telnet.banner.banner

Max buckets 10

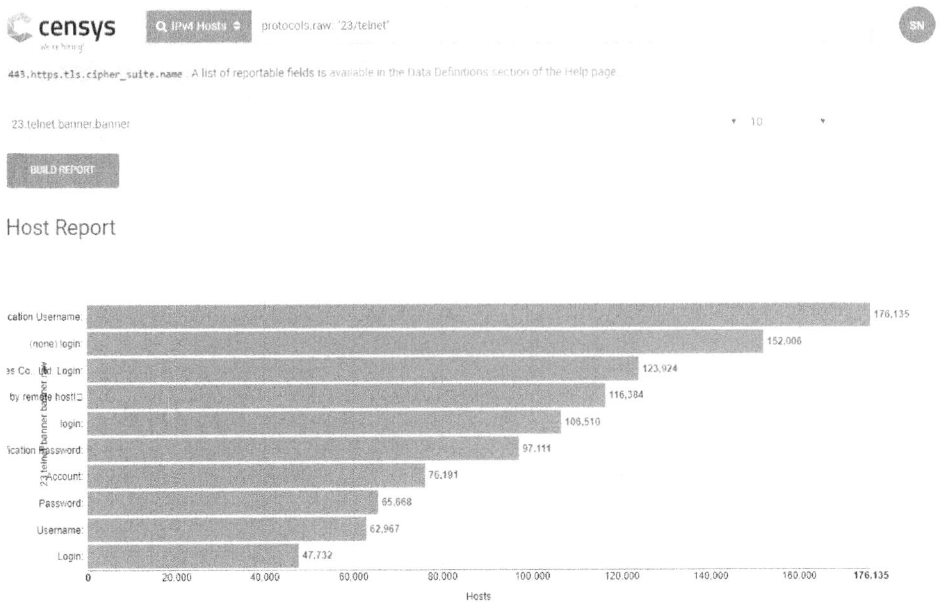

Figure 161 Censys Top Ten report telnet banners

Table 68 Censys Top 10 report 23.telnet.banner.banner

Banner	Number	Percentage
User Access Verification Username:	176,135	5.28%
(none) login:	152,006	4.55%
Welcome Visiting Huawei Home Gateway Copyright by Huawei Technologies Co., Ltd. Login:	123,924	3.71%
%connection closed by remote host!	116,384	3.49%
login:	106,510	3.19%
User Access Verification Password:	97,111	2.91%

Account:	76,191	2.28%
Password:	65,668	1.97%
Username:	62,967	1.89%
Other	2,313,785	69.31%
Total	3,338,413	100.0%

11.12 Find hacked websites

Its handy to find hacked websites and see what damage, groups, tools, techniques used or if systems are unprotected. Quick and dirty dorking search strings can be used and refined.

80.http.get.body: hacked

80.http.get.body: "hacked by"

8080.http.get.body: hacked

8080.http.get.body: "hacked by"

80.http.get.body: "hacker team"

80.http.get.title: hacked

To discover which operating system seems to be hacked the most use the Report Builder or the direct search string

https://censys.io/ipv4/report?q=hacked&field=metadata .os.raw&max_buckets=

Why so many fedora challenge?

Solution, in the html code `<li>Neither the Fedora Project or Red Hat has "hacked" this webserver, this test page is an included component of Apache's httpd webserver software.</li>`

```
Why so many Windows?
Because they were actually hacked
```

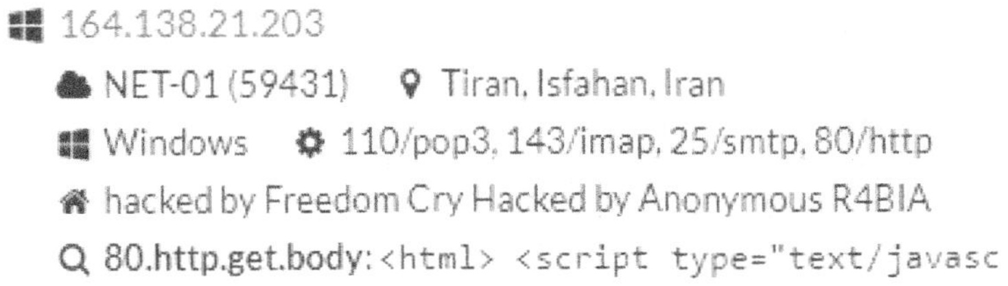

Figure 162 Censys.io (hacked) AND metadata.os: "Windows" search result

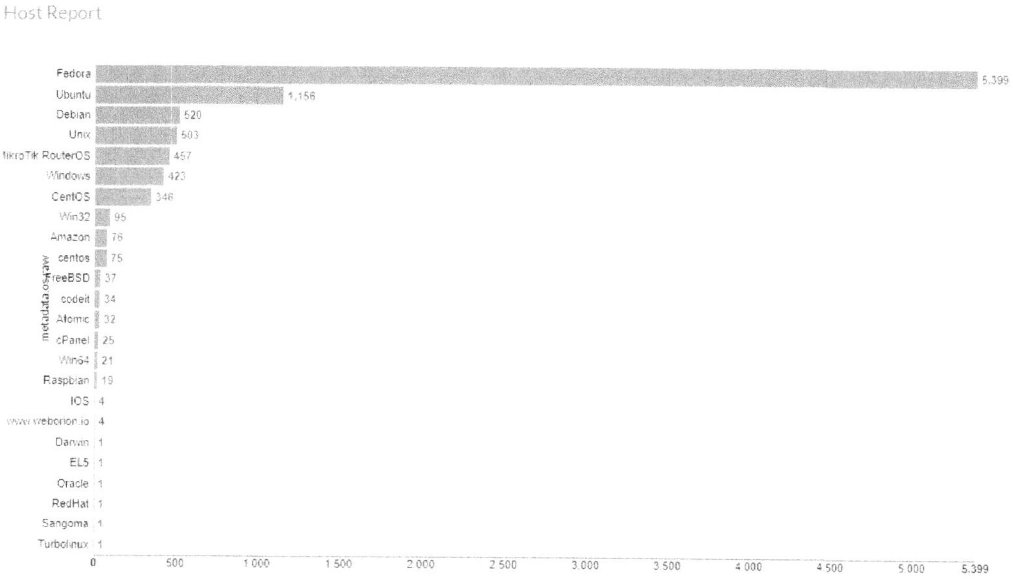

Figure 163 Censys general keyword "hacked" search AND operating system

Table 69 Censys report Hacked and count by operating system 17 November 2017

Metadata.os.raw	Hosts	Percentage
Fedora	5,399	58.48%
Ubuntu	1,156	12.52%
Debian	520	5.63%
Unix	503	5.45%
MikroTik RouterOS	457	4.95%
Windows	423	4.58%

CentOS	346	3.75%
Win32	95	1.03%
Amazon	76	0.82%
centos	75	0.81%
other		
Total	9232	100%

(hacked) AND metadata.os: "Windows" and host report by 80.http.get.title

(hacked) AND metadata.os: "Windows" NOT (80.http.get.title: "Engage" or 80.http.get.title: "Services" or 80.http.get.title: "home")


```
"metadata": { "count": 307, "backend_time": 142,
"nonnull_count": 266, "other_result_count": 147,
"buckets": 50, "error_bound": 0, "query": "(hacked )
AND metadata.os: \"Windows\" NOT (80.http.get.title:
\"Engage\" or 80.http.get.title: \"Services\" or
80.http.get.title: \"home\" or 80.http.get.title:
\"\")"
```


Table 70 Filtered Top Ten report keyword Hacked by Windows OS

80.http.get.title.raw	Hosts
Hacked By Team System Dz	5
Hacked By Syrian Revolution Soldiers #SRS	4

Access Override!!	2
Hacked By International Force	2
Hacked By Turkhacks.Com ~ depres4n - Security	2
Hacked by CapoO_TunisiAnoO	2
LinuXploit_crew	2
Welcome to 缅甸娱乐城官方组委会 - by hackkey hacked!	2
[!] HaCkeD By TRAFIQUANT	2
# Fatal Error Crew ~ Follow us: @FatalErrorSec # Elemento_pcx & s4r4d0 &sup3rm4n ! PWNED YOUR BOX!!!	1

80.http.get.title: "Hacked " or 80.http.get.title: "pwnd"

```
"query": "80.http.get.title: \"Hacked \" or
80.http.get.title: \"pwnd\" "
```

```
10 bucket
```

80.http.get.title.raw	Hosts	Percentage
HackeD By Desert Warriors	105	9.83%
Hacked By GHoST61	40	3.75%
Hacked By TechnicaL	21	1.97%
Hacked By AnonymousFox	17	1.59%

Hacked by D.R.S Dz Team	13	1.22%
Hacked	12	1.12%
[.:.] Hacked By Sid Gifari From BD_LEVEL_7 [.:.]	11	1.03%
HaCked By ReKaN ErrOr	10	0.94%
hacked by GHoST61	10	0.94%
HaCkeD by BALA SNIPER	9	0.84%
Other	820	76.78%
Total	1,068	100.0%

Hacked website HTML Body

```
80.http.get.body
<meta http-equiv="Content-Type" content="text/html;
charset=ISO-8859-1">
<meta name="robots" content="NOINDEX,
NOFOLLOW">
<meta name="description" content="hacked by
budi_spielberg">
<meta name="keyword" content="hacked by budi_spielberg,
hacked, h4ck3d, owned, 0wn3d, defaced, d3f4c3d, by,
budi_spielberg">
<title>:: Hacked by budi_spielberg::</title>
<!--
-
-
- 8888888888888888
- 88888888888888888888888

80.http.get.title
:: Hacked by budi_spielberg::
```

Chapter 12

Censys API & Tools

INFORMATION IN THIS CHAPTER:

- What the Censys API is
- Using the API with Metasploit
- Using the API with Recon NG
- Using the API with SpiderFoot

Yet the deepest truths are best read between the lines, and, for the most part, refuse to be written.

- Amos Bronson Alcott

12 Censys with tools

12.1 Censys API with tools

There are many reasons you might want to use the Censys API with other tools. Getting data into various tool formats, combining data , etc. between tools. All of the tools will use the Jason format and interact with the Censys Rest API. The searches will essentially be the same as using the web search function. You can access the API directly using search queries with both Python and PowerShell.

12.2 Metasploit

Metasploit, the free community edition that comes with Kali, interacts with the Censys API in the same way as a web search.

In your Kali machine, open a terminal session, update, open and start Metasploit

Most of the time to open Metasploit:

root@kali:~# **msfconsole**

Sometimes to open either Metasploit you will need to start the services

root@kali:~# **service postgresql start**

root@kali:~# **service metasploit start**

root@kali:~# **msfconsole**

It is okay most of the time if you get an error after **service metasploit start**

Once Metasploit is started, search for Censys module(s), then go into the options to input your Key and Secret.

Msf > **search censys**

Msf > **use auxiliary/gather/censys_search**

Msf > **show options**

Msf > **set CENSYS-SECRET** [enter your API secret]

Msf > **set CENSYS_UID** [enter your API UID]

```
msf auxiliary(censys_search) > set CENSYS_SECRET XXXXXXX
CENSYS_SECRET => XXXXXXX
msf auxiliary(censys_search) > set CENSYS_UID YYYYYY
CENSYS_UID => YYYYYY
```

Figure 164 Metasploit setting Censys API information

Msf > **show options**

```
Module options (auxiliary/gather/censys_search):

   Name                Current Setting  Required  Description
   ----                ---------------  --------  -----------
   CENSYS_DORK                          yes       The Censys Search Dork
   CENSYS_SEARCHTYPE   certificates     yes       The Censys Search Type (Accepted:
 certificates, ipv4, websites)
   CENSYS_SECRET       XXXXXXX          yes       The Censys API SECRET
   CENSYS_UID          YYYYYY           yes       The Censys API UID
```

Figure 165 Metasploit showing Censys module options

The **CENSYS_DORK**, the keyword search and the **CENSYS_SEARCHTYPE**, either IPv4, certificates or websites is required. The websites is searching in the top Censys websites.

12.3 Metasploit Censys FBI certificate search

In Metasploit, continuing in the Censys module. You will use the keyword of the domain for the FBI and look for certificates containing the domain name. Not all systems are FBI systems.

Msf > **set CENSYS_DORK fbi.gov**

Msf > **set CENSYS_SEARCHTYPE certificates**

Msf > **show options**

```
Module options (auxiliary/gather/censys_search):

   Name                Current Setting  Required  Description
   ----                ---------------  --------  -----------
   CENSYS_DORK         fbi.gov          yes       The Censys Search Dork
   CENSYS_SEARCHTYPE   certificates     yes       The Censys Search Type (Accepted:
 certificates, ipv4, websites)
   CENSYS_SECRET       XXXXXXX          yes       The Censys API SECRET
   CENSYS_UID          YYYYYY           yes       The Censys API UID
```

To search, type **run** and Metasploit will use your Censys API credentials to return the IP address and hostnames.

Msf > **run**

12.4 Recon NG

Four main areas

- Discovery
- Exploitation
- Import
- Recon

12.4.1 Configure Recon-NG

To open, go to Applications, Information Gathering, then Recon-NG. It will pull up a terminal session, but will throw red errors until all the API keys are setup. Disregard the errors, it will load.

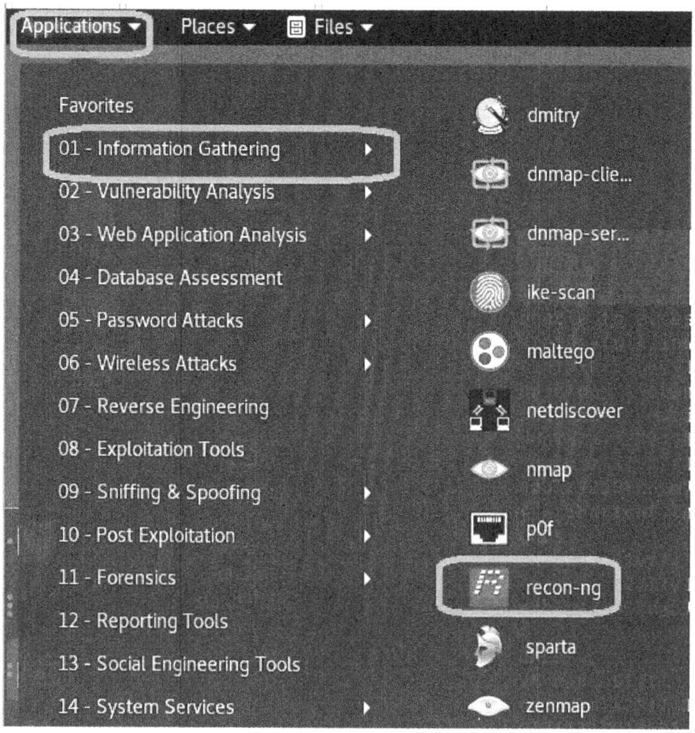

Figure 166 How to open Recon -NG

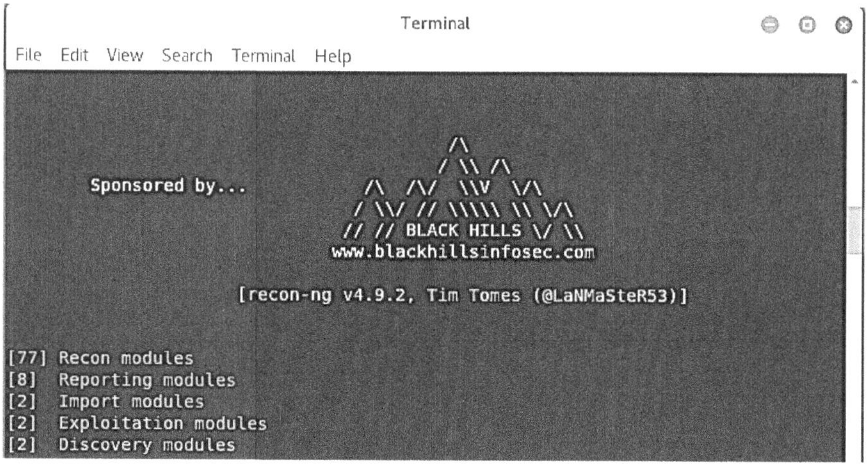

Figure 167 Recon-NG loaded after red errors

We want to change a few options after opening Recon -ng. The application is running in Linux, so we will change the **THREADS** to

255, to try and speed up searches. I enjoy people blaming the Russians, so I tend to change my user agent string to something Putin or Cyrillic language based.

In order to use Recon-NG with Censys, the API Key and the API Secret Key must be added into the application file. First check which keys are installed, then add Censys.io, then we will double check the information was added.

```
recon-ng][default] > keys list
 +--------------------------------------------------------------+
 |      Name      |              Value              |
 +--------------------------------------------------------------+
<snip>
| censysio_id       |                                 |
 | censysio_secret  |                                 |
<snip>
+---------------------------+
[recon-ng][default] > keys add censysio_secret API Secret
Key
[*] Key 'censysio_secret' added.
[recon-ng][default] > keys add censysio_id  API Key
[*] Key 'censysio_id' added.
[recon-ng][default] > show keys
 +--------------------------------------------------------------+
 |      Name      |              Value              |
 +--------------------------------------------------------------+
<snip>
| censysio_id       |        API Key              |
 | censysio_secret  |        API Secret Key       |
<snip>
[recon-ng][default] > set threads 255
THREADS => 255
[recon-ng][default] > set user-agent PutinLovesYou
USER-AGENT => PutinLovesYou
{recon-ng][default] > show options
```

Recon -NG has one built in Censys.io related Censys.io Netblock Enumerator module called Censys.io, located in the Recon section. SQL access to Censys is required, this is different from regular access

Which comes with a regular account. The module settings are displayed by showing information, show info. Some settings might have to be changed depending on your bandwidth. I do not have access to the Censys SQL portion

[recon-ng][default] > **search censys**
[recon-ng][default] > **use recon/netblocks-ports/censysio**
use recon/netblocks-ports/censysio
[recon-ng][default][censysio] > **show info**
Name: Censys.io Netblock Enumerator
Path: modules/recon/netblocks-ports/censysio.py
Author: John Askew (https://bitbucket.org/skew)
Keys: censysio_id, censysio_secret
Description:
 Queries the censys.io API to enumerate information about netblocks.
Options:

Name	Current Value	Required	Description
LIMIT	True	yes	toggle rate limiting
RATE	0.2	yes	search endpoint leak rate (tokens/second)
SOURCE	default	yes	source of input (see 'show info' for details)

Source Options:
 default SELECT DISTINCT netblock FROM netblocks WHERE netblock IS NOT NULL
 <string> string representing a single input
 <path> path to a file containing a list of inputs
 query <sql> database query returning one column of inputs
Comments:
 * To enumerate ports for hosts, use the following query as the

SOURCE option.

- SELECT DISTINCT ip_address || '/32' FROM hosts WHERE ip_address IS NOT NULL

12.4.2 Import Additional Censys modules into Recon NG

Extra modules are at GitHub
https://github.com/scumsec/Recon-ng-modules

- **Built in: Censys.io Netblock Enumerator**
- **recon/companies-hosts/censys_org**
- **recon/domains-hosts/censys_mx**
- **recon/netblocks-ports/censysio**

```
recon/netblocks-ports/census_2012
recon/netblocks-ports/censysio
```

Figure 168 Additional Censys Recon NG modules

12.5 Spiderfoot

Spiderfoot is a great OSINT tool which checks over 100 data sources. Its most accurate the more API keys you can add and data sources you can check. Currently, Spiderfoot can perform general keyword searches with the Censys Rest API module. Not super sexy but module functionality improvements occur frequently. If your target is the FBI.gov, it will return general keyword information then try to combine it with other data sources to both report try to determine if there are any interesting findings.

Chapter 13

Censys API Functionality

INFORMATION IN THIS CHAPTER:

- Censys Rest API Reference
- Rest API functionality

An API that isn't comprehensive isn't usable.

James Gosling

13 Rest API

13.1 The Censys API

Censys' REST API uses programmatic access which provides the same results as the Censys web search. Searches using either method must meet the terms and conditions along with rate limits for you Censys account. The encoded and decoded format is Json.

Be aware, the API Key and Secret are formatted in Base64 Basic when sent to and from Censys. Base64 is decodable including cases where salting, adding or padding false information is applied. The encoding format of Base64 is widespread in many applications.

Reference: **https://censys.io/api/v1/docs/**

13.2 Search

For exposing a single endpoint

POST

Table 71 POST Search Rest API URL Parameters & examples

URL Parameters	Example
/api/v1/search/ipv4	metadata.os: "centos"
/api/v1/search/websites	80.http.get.headers.server: centos
/api/v1/search/certificates	parsed.names: fbi.gov

The data parameters include the required query plus any other options to expand or refine the search. By default, Censys returns one page worth pf results. If you want more, **Page** will return the number of pages you want beyond the default. The **Fields** are an optional strings which you wanted explicitly returned such as, IP address, geolocation information or network information. **Flatten** is an optional Boolean which formats the search results and is on by default.

Table 72 POST Search Rest API Data Parameters

Data Parameter	Type	Required
Query	String	Yes
Page	Integer	No

Fields	List of strings	No
Flatten	Boolean	No

Table 73 POST Search Rest API Response codes

Response code	Description
200	Success
400	Bad request
404	Not Found
405	Method not allowed
429	Rate Limit Exceeded
500	Internal Server Error

Example:
https://censys.io/certificates?q=443.https.tls.certificate.parsed.issuer.organization%09+Honeywell
or with API key & secret
https://censys.io/api/v1/search/certificates?q=443.https.tls.certificate.parsed.issuer.organization%09+Honeywell

Figure 169 HTTP Honeywell certificate organisation

13.3 View

GET

/api/v1/view/ :index/ :id

Table 74 View Rest API GET URL Parameters

URL Parameter	Type	Required
Index	String	Yes

ID	String	Yes

Example:
/api/v1/view/websites/fbi.gov

Table 75 View Rest API GET Response codes

Response code	Description
200	Success
404	Not Found
429	Rate Limit Exceeded
500	Internal Server Error

13.4 Create Report

POST

/api/v1/view/report/ :id

Table 76 Rest API Report URL Parameters

URL Parameter	Example
/api/v1/report/ipv4	80.http.get.body: porn
/api/v1/report/websites	
/api/v1/report/certificates	

Table 77 Rest API Report Index URL Parameter

URL Parameter	Type	Required
Index	String	Yes

Table 78 Rest API Report Data Parameters

Data Parameter	Type	Required
Query	String	Yes

Field	String	Yes
Buckets	Integer	No

Table 79 Rest API Report Response codes

Response code	Description
200	Success
404	Not Found
429	Rate Limit Exceeded
500	Internal Server Error

13.5 Report Query

SQL Query

POST

/api/v1/query

Table 80 Rest API Report Query Data Parameter

Data Parameter	Type	Required
Query	String	Yes

Table 81 Rest API Report Query response codes

Response code	Description
200	Success
404	Not Found
429	Rate Limit Exceeded
500	Internal Server Error

13.5.1 Get Job Status

GET

/api/v1/query/:job_id

Table 82 Rest API Get Job Status URL Parameter

URL Parameter	Type	Required
Job_id	String	Yes

Table 83 Rest API Get Job Status response codes

Response code	Description
200	Success
404	Not Found
429	Rate Limit Exceeded
500	Internal Server Error

13.5.2 Get Job Results

GET
/api/v1/query/:job_id/:page

Table 84 Rest API Get Job Results URL Parameter

URL Parameter	Type	Required
Job_id	String	Yes

Table 85 Rest API Get Job Results response codes

Response code	Description
200	Success
404	Not Found
429	Rate Limit Exceeded
500	Internal Server Error

13.5.3 Get Series

GET

/api/v1/query_definitions

Table 86 Rest API Get Series response code

Response code	Description
200	Success

13.6.4 Get Series Details

GET

/api/v1/query_definitions/:series

Table 87 Rest API Get Series Details URL Parameter

URL Parameter	Type	Required
Series	String	Yes

The values for series are returned from Get Series

Table 88 Rest API Get Series Details response codes

Response code	Description
200	Success
404	Not Found

13.6 Report Export

13.6.1 Start Export Job

Data Parameter	Type	Required
Query	String	
Format	String	
Flatten	Boolean	

Compress	Boolean
Delimiter	CSV only
Headers	CSV only

Response code	Description
200	Success
404	Not Found
429	Rate Limit Exceeded
500	Internal Server Error

13.6.2 Export Get Job Status

GET

/api/v1/export/:job_id

Table 89 Rest API Export Get Job Status URL Parameter

URL Parameter	Type	Required
Job_id	String	Yes

Table 90 Rest API Export Get Job Status response codes

Response code	Description
200	Success
404	Not Found
429	Rate Limit Exceeded
500	Internal Server Error

13.7 Data

13.7.1 Data Get Series

Request-CensysScanTypes
GET

/api/v1/data

Table 91 Rest API Data Get Series response codes

Response code	Description
200	Success
404	Not Found
429	Rate Limit Exceeded
500	Internal Server Error

13.7.2 Data View Series

GET

/api/v1/data/:series

Read-CensysViewSeries

13.7.3 Data View Results

GET

/api/v1/data/:series/:result

Table 92 Rest API Data View Results URL Parameters

URL Parameters	Type	Required
Series	String	Yes
Result	String	Yes

Table 93 Rest API Data View Results response codes

Response code	Description
200	Success
404	Not Found
429	Rate Limit Exceeded
500	Internal Server Error

Read Further

INFORMATION IN THIS CHAPTER:

- Tools
- Books
- ZLINT

How do we change the world? One random act of hacking at a time.

- Morgan Freeman

Resources

Table 94 Additional Tools

URL	Description
https://www.telerik.com/download/fiddler	Fiddler, Windows based proxy application similar but better than Burp
https://tools.hypasec.com	Hypasec tools directory
http://www.chipkin.com/files/resources/modbus/Installer_CAS_Modbus_TCP_Parser.exe	Chipkin Modbus TCP Parser
https://name-fake.com/	Fake name generator

Further reading

Chipkin, Peter. 2009. *Bacnet for Field Technicians.* Vanvouver: Chipkin Automation. **ISBN-13:** 978-1449586492

Chipkin, Peter. 2010. *Modbus for Field Technicians.* Vancouver: Chipkin Automation. **ISBN-13:** 978-1456376444

Kubecka, Chris 2017 *Down the Rabbit Hole An OSINT Journey: Open Source Intelligence Gathering for Penetration Testing* Amsterdam: Hypasec **ISBN-13:** 978-0995687547

Table 95 Censys Basic Parsed Certificate fields

Basic Information
Parsed.names:
Parsed.subject_dn:
Parsed.isser_dn:

Parsed.serial_number:
Parsed.subject_dn:

Table 96 Censys Parsed Fingerprint fields

Fingerprint
Parsed.fingerprint_sha256:
Parsed.fingerprint_sha1:
Parsed.fingerprint_md5:
Parsed.spki_subject_fingerprint:
Parsed.tbs_fingerprint:
Parsed.tbs_noct_fingerprint:

Table 97 Censys Apple Certificate Validation fields

Apple Validation
Validation.apple.valid:
Validation.apple.was_valid:
Validation.apple.trusted_path:
Validation.apple.had_trusted_path:
Validation.apple.type:
Validation.apple.paths:
Validation.apple.parents:

Table 98 Censys NSS Firefox Validation Certificate fields

NSS Firefox Validation
Validation.nss.valid:
Validation.nss.was_valid:
Validation.nss.trusted_path:
Validation.nss.had_trusted_path:
Validation.nss.type:
Validation.nss.paths:
Validation.nss.parents:

Table 99 Censys Google Certificate Transparency Validation fields

Google CT Validation
Validation.google_ct_primary.valid:
Validation.google_ct_primary.was_valid:
Validation.google_ct_primary.trusted_path:
Validation.google_ct_primary.had_trusted_path:
Validation.google_ct_primary.type:
Validation.google_ct_primary.paths:
Validation.google_ct_primary.parents:

Table 100 Censys Parsed Validity fields

Validity Period

Parsed.validity.start:
Parsed.validity.end:
Parsed.validity.length:

Table 101 Censys Parsed Subject fields

Subject
Parsed.subject.common_name:
Parsed.subject.common_name.raw:
Parsed.subject.email_address:
Parsed.subject.email_address.raw
Parsed.subject.province:
Parsed.subject.province.raw:
Parsed.subject.organization:
Parsed.subject.organization.raw:
Parsed.subject.organizational_unit:
Parsed.subject.organizational_unit.raw:
Parsed.subject.country:
Parsed.subject.country.raw:
Parsed.subject.serial_number:
Parsed.subject.locaity:
Parsed.subject.locality.raw:

Parsed.subject.domain_component:
Parsed.subject.domain_component.raw:
Parsed.subject.street_address:
Parsed.subject.street_address.raw:
Parsed.subject.postal_code:

Table 102 Censys Parsed Issuer fields

Issuer
Parsed.issuer.province:
Parsed.issuer.province.raw:
Parsed.issuer.organization:
Parsed.issuer.organization.raw:
Parsed.issuer.organizational_unit:
Parsed.issuer.organizational_unit.raw:
Parsed.issuer.country:
Parsed.issuer.country.raw:
Parsed.issuer.common_name:
Parsed.issuer.common_name.raw:
Parsed.issuer.email_address:
Parsed.issuer.email_address.raw:
Parsed.issuer.serial_number:

Parsed.issuer.locality:
Parsed.issuer.locality.raw:
Parsed.issuer.domain_component:
Parsed.issuer.domain_component.raw:
Parsed.issuer.street_address:
Parsed.issuer.street_address.raw:
Parsed.issuer.postal_code:

Table 103 Censys Parsed Certificate Public Key fields

Public Key
Parsed.subject_key_info.fingerprint_sha256:
Parsed.subject_key_info.key_algorithm.oid:
Parsed.subject_key_info.key_algorithm.name:
Parsed.subject_key_info.edcsa_public_key.b:
Parsed.subject_key_info.edcsa_public_key.gy:
Parsed.subject_key_info.edcsa_public_key.n:
Parsed.subject_key_info.edcsa_public_key.p:
Parsed.subject_key_info.edcsa_public_key.y:
Parsed.subject_key_info.edcsa_public_key.x:
Parsed.subject_key_info.edcsa_public_key.gx:
Parsed.subject_key_info.rsa_public_key.length:

Parsed.subject_key_info. rsa_public_key.modulus:
Parsed.subject_key_info. rsa_public_key.exponent:
Parsed.subject_key_info.dsa_public_key.q:
Parsed.subject_key_info. dsa_public_key.p:
Parsed.subject_key_info. dsa_public_key.y:
Parsed.subject_key_info. dsa_public_key.g:

Table 104 Censys Parsed Certificate Miscellaneous fields

Misc
Parsed.version:
Parents:
Precert:
Parsed.validation_level:
Parsed.redacted:

Table 105 Censys Parsed Certificate SAN fields

Subject Alternative Names (SANs)
Parsed.extensions.subject_alt_name.dns_names:
Parsed.extensions.subject_alt_name.ip_addresses:
Parsed.extensions.subject_alt_name.email_addresses:
Parsed.extensions.subject_alt_name.edi_party_names.name_assigner:
Parsed.extensions.subject_alt_name.edi_party_names.p

arty_name:
Parsed.extensions.subject_alt_name.other_names.id:
Parsed.extensions.subject_alt_name.other_names.value:
Parsed.extensions.subject_alt_name.registered_ids:
Parsed.extensions.subject_alt_name.uniform_resource_identifiers:
Parsed.extensions.subject_alt_name.uniform_resource_identifiers.raw:
Parsed.extensions.subject_alt_name.directory_names.serial_number:
Parsed.extensions.subject_alt_name.directory_names.serial_number.raw:
Parsed.extensions.subject_alt_name.directory_names.common_name:
Parsed.extensions.subject_alt_name.directory_names.common_name.raw
Parsed.extensions.subject_alt_name.directory_names.country:
Parsed.extensions.subject_alt_name.directory_names.raw:
Parsed.extensions.subject_alt_name.directory_names.locality:
Parsed.extensions.subject_alt_name.directory_names.locality.raw:
Parsed.extensions.subject_alt_name.directory_names.pr

ovince:
Parsed.extensions.subject_alt_name.directory_names.province.raw:
Parsed.extensions.subject_alt_name.directory_names.street_address:
Parsed.extensions.subject_alt_name.directory_names.street_address.raw:
Parsed.extensions.subject_alt_name.directory_names.organization:
Parsed.extensions.subject_alt_name.directory_names.organizational_unit:
Parsed.extensions.subject_alt_name.directory_names.organizational_unit.raw:
Parsed.extensions.subject_alt_name.directory_names.postal_code:
Parsed.extensions.subject_alt_name.directory_names.domain_component:
Parsed.extensions.subject_alt_name.directory_names.domain_component.raw:

Table 106 Censys Parsed Certificate Basic Constraints fields

Basic Constraints
Parsed.extensions.basic_contraints.max_path_len:
Parsed.extensions. basic_contraints.is_ca:

Table 107 Censys Parsed Key Usage fields

Key Usage
Parsed.extensions.key_usage.encipher_only:
Parsed.extensions.key_usage.certificate_sign:
Parsed.extensions.key_usage.key_encipherment:
Parsed.extensions.key_usage.digital_signature:
Parsed.extensions.key_usage.content_commitment:
Parsed.extensions.key_usage.decipher_only:
Parsed.extensions.key_usage.key_agreement:
Parsed.extensions.key_usage.data_encipherment:
Parsed.extensions.key_usage.crl_sign:
Parsed.extensions.key_usage.value:

Table 108 Censys Parsed Certificate Extended Key Usage field

Extended Key Usage
Parsed.extensions.extended+key_usage:

Table 109 Censys Parsed Certificate SKID field

Subject Key ID (SKID)
Parsed.extensions.subject_key_id:

Table 110 Censys Parsed Certificate AKID field

Authority Key ID (AKID)
Parsed.extensions.authority_key_id:

Table 111 Censys Parsed Certificate AIA field

Authority Info Access (AIA)
Parsed.extensions.authority_info_access.ocsp_urls:
Parsed.extensions.authority_info_access.ocsp_urls.raw:
Parsed.extensions.authority_info_access.issuer_urls:
Parsed.extensions.authority_info_access.issuer_urls.raw :

Table 112 Censys Certificate Policy fields

Certificate Policies
Parsed.extensions.certificate_policies.id:
Parsed.extensions.certificate_policies.name:
Parsed.extensions.certificate_policies.cps:
Parsed.extensions.certificate_policies.user_notice.explicit_text:
Parsed.extensions.certificate_policies.user_notice.notice_reference.organization:
Parsed.extensions.certificate_policies.user_notice.notice_reference.notice_numbers:

Table 113Censys Parsed Certificate Control fields

CRL Distribution Points
Parsed.extensions.crl_distribution_points:

Table 114 Censys Parsed Certificate Transparency Poison fields

Embedded SCTS/CT Poison
Parsed.extensions.certificate_timestamps.log_id:
Parsed.extensions.certificate_timestamps.timestamp:
Parsed.extensions.certificate_timestamps.version:
Parsed.extensions.certificate_timestamps.extentions:
Parsed.extensions.ct.poison:

Table 115 Censys Parsed Certificate Name Constraints fields

Name Constraints
Parsed.extensions.name_constraints.permitted_names:
Parsed.extensions.name_constraints.permitted_names.raw:
Parsed.extensions.name_constraints.permitted_ip_addresses.cidr:
Parsed.extensions.name_constraints.permitted_ip_addresses.begin:
Parsed.extensions.name_constraints.permitted_ip_addresses.end:
Parsed.extensions.name_constraints.permitted_ip_addr

esses.mask:
Parsed.extensions.name_constraints.permitted_directory_names.province:
Parsed.extensions.name_constraints.permitted_directory_names.province.raw:
Parsed.extensions.name_constraints.permitted_directory_names.organization:
Parsed.extensions.name_constraints.permitted_directory_names.organization.raw:
Parsed.extensions.name_constraints.permitted_directory_names.organizational_unit:
Parsed.extensions.name_constraints.permitted_directory_names.organizational_unit.raw:
Parsed.extensions.name_constraints.permitted_directory_names.country:
Parsed.extensions.name_constraints.permitted_directory_names.country.raw:
Parsed.extensions.name_constraints.permitted_directory_names.common_name:
Parsed.extensions.name_constraints.permitted_directory_names.common_name.raw:
Parsed.extensions.name_constraints.permitted_directory_names.serial_number:
Parsed.extensions.name_constraints.permitted_directory_names.locality:
Parsed.extensions.name_constraints.permitted_director

y_names.locality.raw:
Parsed.extensions.name_constraints.permitted_directory_names.domain_component:
Parsed.extensions.name_constraints.permitted_directory_names.domain_component.raw:
Parsed.extensions.name_constraints.permitted_directory_names.street_address:
Parsed.extensions.name_constraints.permitted_directory_names.street_address.raw:
Parsed.extensions.name_constraints.permitted_directory_names.postal_code:
Parsed.extensions.name_constraints.permitted_email_addresses:
Parsed.extensions.name_constraints. permitted_email_addresses.raw:
Parsed.extensions.name_constraints.excluded__names:
Parsed.extensions.name_constraints.excluded_names.raw:
Parsed.extensions.name_constraints.excluded_ip_addesses.cidr:
Parsed.extensions.name_constraints.excluded_ip_addresses.begin
Parsed.extensions.name_constraints.excluded_ip_addresses.end:
Parsed.extensions.name_constraints.excluded_ip_addresses.mask:

Parsed.extensions.name_constraints.excluded_email_addresses:
Parsed.extensions.name_constraints.excluded_email_addresses.raw:
Parsed.extensions.name_constraints.excluded_directory_names:
Parsed.extensions.name_constraints.excluded_directory_names.province:
Parsed.extensions.name_constraints.excluded_directory_names.provence.raw:
Parsed.extensions.name_constraints.excluded_directory_names.organization:
Parsed.extensions.name_constraints.excluded_directory_names.organization.raw:
Parsed.extensions.name_constraints.excluded_directory_names.organizational_unit:
Parsed.extensions.name_constraints.excluded_directory_names.organizational_unit.raw:
Parsed.extensions.name_constraints.excluded_directory_names.country:
Parsed.extensions.name_constraints.excluded_directory_names.country.raw:
Parsed.extensions.name_constraints.excluded_directory_names.common_name:
Parsed.extensions.name_constraints.excluded_directory_names.common_name.raw:

Parsed.extensions.name_constraints.excluded_directory_names.serial_number:
Parsed.extensions.name_constraints.excluded_directory_names.locality:
Parsed.extensions.name_constraints.excluded_directory_names.locality.raw:
Parsed.extensions.name_constraints.excluded_directory_names.domain_component:
Parsed.extensions.name_constraints.excluded_directory_names.domain.component.raw:
Parsed.extensions.name_constraints.excluded_directory_names.stree_address:
Parsed.extensions.name_constraints.excluded_directory_names.street_address.raw:
Parsed.extensions.name_constraints.excluded_directory_names.postal_code:
Parsed.extensions.name_constraints.critical:

Table 116 Censys Parsed Certificate Unknown fields

Unknown Extensions
Parsed.unknown_extensions.critical:
Parsed.unknown_extensions.id:
Parsed.unknown_extensions.value:

Table 117 Censys Parsed Signature fields

Signature
Parsed.signature.self_signed:
Parsed.signature.value:
Parsed.signature.signature_algorithm.oid:
Parsed.signature. signature_algorithm.name:

Table 118 Censys Certificate Metadata fields

Metadata
Metadata.updates_at:
Metadata.added_at:
Metadata.post_processed:
Metadata.post_processed_at:
Metadata.seen_in_scan:
Metadata.source:
Metadata.parse_status:
Metadata.parse_version:
Metadata.parse_error:

Table 119 Censys CCADB Audit fields

CCADB Audit

audit.ccadb.owner_name:
audit.ccadb.parent_name:
audit.ccadb.certificate_name:
audit.ccadb.certificate_policy:
audit.ccadb.certifcation_oractice_statement:
audit.ccadb.cp_same_as_parent:
audit.ccadb.audit_same_as_parent:
audit.ccadb.standard_audit:
audit.ccadb.cr_audit:
audit.ccadb.auditor:
audit.ccadb.standard_audit_statement_timestamp:
audit.ccadb.management_assertions_by:
audit.ccadb.comments:
audit.ccadb.ev_policy_oids:
audit.ccadb.approval_bug:
audit.ccadb.first_nss_release:
audit.ccadb.first_firefox_release:
audit.ccadb.test_website_valid:
audit.ccadb.mozilla_applied_constraints:
audit.ccadb.company_website:
audit.ccadb.geographic_focus:

audit.ccadb.standard_audit_type:
audit.ccadb.current_in_intermediates:
audit.ccadb.current_in_roots:

Certificate Transparency Logs
ct.cnnic_ctserver.index:
ct.cnnic_ctserver.censys_to_ct_at:
ct.cnnic_ctserver.ct_to_censys_at:
ct.cnnic_ctserver.added_to_ct_at:
ct.gdca_ct.index:
ct.gdca_ct.censys_to_ct_at:
ct.gdca_ct.ct_to_censys_at:
ct.gdca_ct.added_to_ct_at:
ct.izenpe_eus_ct.index:
ct.izenpe_eus_ct.censys_to_ct_at:
ct.izenpe_eus_ct.ct_to_censys_at:
ct.izenpe_eus_ct.added_to_ct_at:
ct.izenpe_com_ct.index:
ct.izenpe_com_ct.censys_to_ct_at:
ct.izenpe_com_ct.ct_to_censys_at:
ct.izenpe_com_ct.added_to_ct_at:

ct.google_aviator.index:
ct.google_aviator.censys_to_ct_at:
ct.google_aviator.ct_to_censys_at:
ct.google_aviator.added_to_ct_at:
ct.izenpe_com_ct.index:
ct.izenpe_com_ct.censys_to_ct_at:
ct.izenpe_com_ct.ct_to_censys_at:
ct.izenpe_com_ct.added_to_ct_at:
ct.google_pilot.index:
ct.google_pilot.censys_to_ct_at:
ct.google_pilot.ct_to_censys_at:
ct.google_pilot.added_to_ct_at:
ct.symantec_ws_deneb.index:
ct.symantec_ws_deneb.censys_to_ct_at:
ct.symantec_ws_deneb.ct_to_censys_at:
ct.symantec_ws_deneb.added_to_ct_at:
ct.digicert_ct1.index:
ct.digicert_ct1.censys_to_ct_at:
ct.digicert_ct1.ct_to_censys_at:
ct.digicert_ct1.added_to_ct_at:
ct.digicert_ct2.index:

ct.digicert_ct2.censys_to_ct_at:
ct.digicert_ct2.ct_to_censys_at:
ct.venafi_api_ctlog.index:
ct.venafi_api_ctlog.censys_to_ct_at:
ct.venafi_api_ctlog.ct_to_censys_at:
ct.venafi_api_ctlog.added_to_ct_at:
ct.censys_dev.index:
ct.censys_dev.censys_to_ct_at:
ct.censys_dev.ct_to_censys_at:
ct.censys_dev.added_to_ct_at:
ct.google_rocketeer.index:
ct.google_rocketeer.censys_to_ct_at:
ct.google_rocketeer.ct_to_censys_at:
ct.google_rocketeer.added_to_ct_at:
ct.google_skydiver.index:
ct.google_skydiver.censys_to_ct_at:
ct.google_skydiver.ct_to_censys_at:
ct.google_skydiver.added_to_ct_at:
ct.google_testtube.index:
ct.google_testtube.censys_to_ct_at:
ct.google_testtube.ct_to_censys_at:

ct.google_testtube.added_to_ct_at:
ct.wosign_ct.index:
ct.wosign_ct.censys_to_ct_at:
ct.wosign_ct.ct_to_censys_at:
ct.wosign_ct.added_to_ct_at:
ct.wosign_ctlog.index:
ct.wosign_ctlog.censys_to_ct_at:
ct.wosign_ctlog.ct_to_censys_at:
ct.wosign_ctlog.added_to_ct_at:
ct.certly_log.index:
ct.certly_log.censys_to_ct_at:
ct.certly_log.ct_to_censys_at:
ct.certly_log.added_to_ct_at:
ct.startssl_ct.index:
ct.startssl_ct.censys_to_ct_at:
ct.startssl_ct.ct_to_censys_at:
ct.startssl_ct.added_to_ct_at:
ct.symantec_ws_sirius.index:
ct.symantec_ws_sirius.censys_to_ct_at:
ct.symantec_ws_sirius.ct_to_censys_at:
ct.symantec_ws_sirius.added_to_ct_at:

ct.symantec_ws_vega.index:	
ct.symantec_ws_vega.censys_to_ct_at:	
ct.symantec_ws_vega.ct_to_censys_at:	
ct.symantec_ws_vega.added_to_ct_at:	
ct.nordu_ct_plausible.index:	
ct.nordu_ct_plausible.censys_to_ct_at:	
ct.nordu_ct_plausible.ct_to_censys_at:	
ct.nordu_ct_plausible.added_to_ct_at:	
ct.google_submariner.index:	
ct.google_submariner.censys_to_ct_at:	
ct.google_submariner.ct_to_censys_at:	
ct.google_submariner.added_to_ct_at:	
ct.google_daedalus.index:	
ct.google_daedalus.censys_to_ct_at:	
ct.google_daedalus.ct_to_censys_at:	
ct.google_daedalus.added_to_ct_at:	
ct.google_icarus.index:	
ct.google_icarus.censys_to_ct_at:	
ct.google_icarus.ct_to_censys_at:	
ct.google_icarus.added_to_ct_at:	
ct.symantec_ws_ct.index:	

ct.symantec_ws_ct.censys_to_ct_at:
ct.symantec_ws_ct.ct_to_censys_at:
ct.symantec_ws_ct.added_to_ct_at:
ct.comodo_dodo.index:
ct.comodo_dodo.censys_to_ct_at:
ct.comodo_dodo.ct_to_censys_at:
ct.comodo_dodo.added_to_ct_at:
ct.comodo_mammoth.index:
ct.comodo_mammoth.censys_to_ct_at:
ct.comodo_mammoth.ct_to_censys_at:
ct.comodo_mammoth.added_to_ct_at:
ct.comodo_sabre.index:
ct.comodo_sabre.censys_to_ct_at:
ct.comodo_sabre.ct_to_censys_at:
ct.comodo_sabre.added_to_ct_at:

Table 120 ZLint

ZLint
zlint.errors_present:
zlint.fatals_present:
zlint.notices_present:

zlint.warnings_present:	
zlint.version:	
zlint.lints.e_basic_constraints_not_critical:	
zlint.lints.e_ca_common_name_missing:	
zlint.lints.e_ca_country_name_invalid:	
zlint.lints.e_ca_country_name_missing:	
zlint.lints.e_ca_crl_sign_not_set:	
zlint.lints.e_ca_is_ca:	
zlint.lints.e_ca_key_cert_sign_not_set:	
zlint.lints.e_ca_key_usage_missing:	
zlint.lints.e_ca_key_usage_not_critical:	
zlint.lints.e_ca_organization_name_missing:	
zlint.lints.e_ca_subject_field_empty:	
zlint.lints.e_cab_dv_conflicts_with_locality:	
zlint.lints.e_cab_dv_conflicts_with_org:	
zlint.lints.e_cab_dv_conflicts_with_postal:	
zlint.lints.e_cab_dv_conflicts_with_province:	
zlint.lints.e_cab_dv_conflicts_with_street:	
zlint.lints.e_cab_iv_requires_personal_name:	
zlint.lints.e_cab_ov_requires_org:	
zlint.lints.e_cert_contains_unique_identifier:	

zlint.lints.e_cert_extensions_version_not_3:
zlint.lints.e_cert_policy_iv_requires_country:
zlint.lints.e_cert_policy_iv_requires_province_or_localit y:
zlint.lints.e_cert_policy_ov_requires_country:
zlint.lints.e_cert_policy_ov_requires_province_or_localit y:
zlint.lints.e_cert_unique_identifier_version_not_2_or_3:
zlint.lints.e_distribution_point_incomplete:
zlint.lints.e_dnsname_bad_character_in_label:
zlint.lints.e_dnsname_contains_bare_iana_suffix:
zlint.lints.e_dnsname_empty_label:
zlint.lints.e_dnsname_hyphen_in_sld:
zlint.lints.e_dnsname_label_too_long:
zlint.lints.e_dnsname_left_label_wildcard_correct:
zlint.lints.e_dnsname_not_valid_tld:
zlint.lints.e_dnsname_underscore_in_sld:
zlint.lints.e_dnsname_wildcard_only_in_left_label:
zlint.lints.e_dsa_correct_order_in_subgroup:
zlint.lints.e_dsa_improper_modulus_or_divisor_size:
zlint.lints.e_dsa_params_missing:
zlint.lints.e_dsa_shorter_than_2048_bits:

zlint.lints.e_dsa_unique_correct_representation:
zlint.lints.e_ec_improper_curves:
zlint.lints.e_ev_business_category_missing:
zlint.lints.e_ev_country_name_missing:
zlint.lints.e_ev_locality_name_missing:
zlint.lints.e_ev_organization_name_missing:
zlint.lints.e_ev_serial_number_missing:
zlint.lints.e_ev_valid_time_too_long:
zlint.lints.e_ext_aia_marked_critical:
zlint.lints.e_ext_authority_key_identifier_critical:
zlint.lints.e_ext_authority_key_identifier_missing:
zlint.lints.e_ext_authority_key_identifier_no_key_identifier:
zlint.lints.e_ext_cert_policy_disallowed_any_policy_qualifier:
zlint.lints.e_ext_cert_policy_duplicate:
zlint.lints.e_ext_cert_policy_explicit_text_ia5_string:
zlint.lints.e_ext_cert_policy_explicit_text_too_long:
zlint.lints.e_ext_duplicate_extension:
zlint.lints.e_ext_freshest_crl_marked_critical:
zlint.lints.e_ext_ian_dns_not_ia5_string:
zlint.lints.e_ext_ian_empty_name:

zlint.lints.e_ext_ian_no_entries:
zlint.lints.e_ext_ian_rfc822_format_invalid:
zlint.lints.e_ext_ian_space_dns_name:
zlint.lints.e_ext_ian_uri_format_invalid:
zlint.lints.e_ext_ian_uri_host_not_fqdn_or_ip:
zlint.lints.e_ext_ian_uri_not_ia5:
zlint.lints.e_ext_ian_uri_relative:
zlint.lints.e_ext_key_usage_cert_sign_without_ca:
zlint.lints.e_ext_key_usage_without_bits:
zlint.lints.e_ext_name_constraints_not_critical:
zlint.lints.e_ext_name_constraints_not_in_ca:
zlint.lints.e_ext_policy_constraints_empty:
zlint.lints.e_ext_policy_constraints_not_critical:
zlint.lints.e_ext_policy_map_any_policy:
zlint.lints.e_ext_san_contains_reserved_ip:
zlint.lints.e_ext_san_directory_name_present:
zlint.lints.e_ext_san_dns_name_too_long:
zlint.lints.e_ext_san_dns_not_ia5_string:
zlint.lints.e_ext_san_edi_party_name_present:
zlint.lints.e_ext_san_empty_name:
zlint.lints.e_ext_san_missing:

zlint.lints.e_ext_san_no_entries:
zlint.lints.e_ext_san_not_critical_without_subject:
zlint.lints.e_ext_san_other_name_present:
zlint.lints.e_ext_san_registered_id_present:
zlint.lints.e_ext_san_rfc822_format_invalid:
zlint.lints.e_ext_san_rfc822_name_present:
zlint.lints.e_ext_san_space_dns_name:
zlint.lints.e_ext_san_uniform_resource_identifier_present:
zlint.lints.e_ext_san_uri_format_invalid:
zlint.lints.e_ext_san_uri_host_not_fqdn_or_ip:
zlint.lints.e_ext_san_uri_not_ia5:
zlint.lints.e_ext_san_uri_relative:
zlint.lints.e_ext_subject_directory_attr_critical:
zlint.lints.e_ext_subject_key_identifier_critical:
zlint.lints.e_ext_subject_key_identifier_missing_ca:
zlint.lints.e_generalized_time_does_not_include_seconds:
zlint.lints.e_generalized_time_includes_fraction_seconds:
zlint.lints.e_generalized_time_not_in_zulu:
zlint.lints.e_ian_bare_wildcard:

zlint.lints.e_ian_dns_name_includes_null_char:
zlint.lints.e_ian_dns_name_starts_with_period:
zlint.lints.e_ian_wildcard_not_first:
zlint.lints.e_inhibit_any_policy_not_critical:
zlint.lints.e_international_dns_name_not_nfkc:
zlint.lints.e_international_dns_name_not_unicode:
zlint.lints.e_invalid_certificate_version:
zlint.lints.e_issuer_field_empty:
zlint.lints.e_name_constraint_empty:
zlint.lints.e_name_constraint_maximum_not_absent:
zlint.lints.e_name_constraint_minimum_non_zero:
zlint.lints.e_old_root_ca_rsa_mod_less_than_2048_bits:
zlint.lints.e_old_sub_ca_rsa_mod_less_than_1024_bits:
zlint.lints.e_old_sub_cert_rsa_mod_less_than_1024_bits:
zlint.lints.e_path_len_constraint_improperly_included:
zlint.lints.e_path_len_constraint_zero_or_less:
zlint.lints.e_public_key_type_not_allowed:
zlint.lints.e_root_ca_extended_key_usage_present:
zlint.lints.e_root_ca_key_usage_must_be_critical:
zlint.lints.e_root_ca_key_usage_present:
zlint.lints.e_rsa_exp_negative:

zlint.lints.e_rsa_mod_less_than_2048_bits:
zlint.lints.e_rsa_no_public_key:
zlint.lints.e_rsa_public_exponent_not_odd:
zlint.lints.e_rsa_public_exponent_too_small:
zlint.lints.e_san_bare_wildcard:
zlint.lints.e_san_dns_name_includes_null_char:
zlint.lints.e_san_dns_name_starts_with_period:
zlint.lints.e_san_wildcard_not_first:
zlint.lints.e_serial_number_longer_than_20_octets:
zlint.lints.e_serial_number_not_positive:
zlint.lints.e_signature_algorithm_not_supported:
zlint.lints.e_sub_ca_aia_does_not_contain_ocsp_url:
zlint.lints.e_sub_ca_aia_marked_critical:
zlint.lints.e_sub_ca_aia_missing:
zlint.lints.e_sub_ca_certificate_policies_missing:
zlint.lints.e_sub_ca_crl_distribution_points_does_not_contain_url:
zlint.lints.e_sub_ca_crl_distribution_points_marked_critical:
zlint.lints.e_sub_ca_crl_distribution_points_missing:
zlint.lints.e_sub_ca_eku_missing:
zlint.lints.e_sub_ca_eku_name_constraints:

zlint.lints.e_sub_ca_must_not_contain_any_policy:
zlint.lints.e_sub_cert_aia_does_not_contain_ocsp_url:
zlint.lints.e_sub_cert_aia_marked_critical:
zlint.lints.e_sub_cert_aia_missing:
zlint.lints.e_sub_cert_cert_policy_empty:
zlint.lints.e_sub_cert_certificate_policies_missing:
zlint.lints.e_sub_cert_country_name_must_appear:
zlint.lints.e_sub_cert_crl_distribution_points_does_not_contain_url:
zlint.lints.e_sub_cert_crl_distribution_points_marked_critical:
zlint.lints.e_sub_cert_eku_missing:
zlint.lints.e_sub_cert_eku_server_auth_client_auth_missing:
zlint.lints.e_sub_cert_given_name_surname_contains_correct_policy:
zlint.lints.e_sub_cert_key_usage_cert_sign_bit_set:
zlint.lints.e_sub_cert_key_usage_crl_sign_bit_set:
zlint.lints.e_sub_cert_locality_name_must_appear:
zlint.lints.e_sub_cert_locality_name_must_not_appear:
zlint.lints.e_sub_cert_not_is_ca:
zlint.lints.e_sub_cert_or_sub_ca_using_sha1:

zlint.lints.e_sub_cert_postal_code_must_not_appear:
zlint.lints.e_sub_cert_province_must_appear:
zlint.lints.e_sub_cert_province_must_not_appear:
zlint.lints.e_sub_cert_street_address_should_not_exist:
zlint.lints.e_sub_cert_valid_time_too_long:
zlint.lints.e_subject_common_name_max_length:
zlint.lints.e_subject_common_name_not_from_san:
zlint.lints.e_subject_contains_noninformational_value:
zlint.lints.e_subject_contains_reserved_ip:
zlint.lints.e_subject_country_not_iso:
zlint.lints.e_subject_empty_without_san:
zlint.lints.e_subject_info_access_marked_critical:
zlint.lints.e_subject_locality_name_max_length:
zlint.lints.e_subject_not_dn:
zlint.lints.e_subject_organization_name_max_length:
zlint.lints.e_subject_organizational_unit_name_max_length:
zlint.lints.e_subject_state_name_max_length:
zlint.lints.e_utc_time_does_not_include_seconds:
zlint.lints.e_utc_time_not_in_zulu:
zlint.lints.e_validity_time_not_positive:

zlint.lints.e_wrong_time_format_pre2050:
zlint.lints.n_ca_digital_signature_not_set:
zlint.lints.n_contains_redacted_dnsname:
zlint.lints.n_sub_ca_eku_not_technically_constrained:
zlint.lints.n_subject_common_name_included:
zlint.lints.w_distribution_point_missing_ldap_or_uri:
zlint.lints.w_dnsname_underscore_in_trd:
zlint.lints.w_dnsname_wildcard_left_of_public_suffix:
zlint.lints.w_eku_critical_improperly:
zlint.lints.w_ext_aia_access_location_missing:
zlint.lints.w_ext_cert_policy_contains_noticeref:
zlint.lints.w_ext_cert_policy_explicit_text_includes_con trol:
zlint.lints.w_ext_cert_policy_explicit_text_not_nfc:
zlint.lints.w_ext_cert_policy_explicit_text_not_utf8:
zlint.lints.w_ext_crl_distribution_marked_critical:
zlint.lints.w_ext_ian_critical:
zlint.lints.w_ext_key_usage_not_critical:
zlint.lints.w_ext_policy_map_not_critical:
zlint.lints.w_ext_policy_map_not_in_cert_policy:
zlint.lints.w_ext_san_critical_with_subject_dn:
zlint.lints.w_ext_subject_key_identifier_missing_sub_ce

rt:
zlint.lints.w_ian_iana_pub_suffix_empty:
zlint.lints.w_issuer_dn_leading_whitespace:
zlint.lints.w_issuer_dn_trailing_whitespace:
zlint.lints.w_multiple_issuer_rdn:
zlint.lints.w_multiple_subject_rdn:
zlint.lints.w_name_constraint_on_edi_party_name:
zlint.lints.w_name_constraint_on_registered_id:
zlint.lints.w_name_constraint_on_x400:
zlint.lints.w_root_ca_basic_constraints_path_len_constraint_field_present:
zlint.lints.w_root_ca_contains_cert_policy:
zlint.lints.w_rsa_mod_factors_smaller_than_752:
zlint.lints.w_rsa_mod_not_odd:
zlint.lints.w_rsa_public_exponent_not_in_range:
zlint.lints.w_san_iana_pub_suffix_empty:
zlint.lints.w_serial_number_low_entropy:
zlint.lints.w_sub_ca_aia_does_not_contain_issuing_ca_url:
zlint.lints.w_sub_ca_certificate_policies_marked_critical:
zlint.lints.w_sub_ca_eku_critical:

zlint.lints.w_sub_ca_name_constraints_not_critical:
zlint.lints.w_sub_cert_aia_does_not_contain_issuing_ca_url:
zlint.lints.w_sub_cert_certificate_policies_marked_critical:
zlint.lints.w_sub_cert_eku_extra_values:
zlint.lints.w_sub_cert_sha1_expiration_too_long:
zlint.lints.w_subject_dn_leading_whitespace:
zlint.lints.w_subject_dn_trailing_whitespace:

Citations & works used

Bibliography

AgnesSmedley. 2017. *Spy*. 18 February. https://www.brainyquote.com/quotes/keywords/spy.html.

Atkins, Christopher. 2016. *Hacking SCADA/Industrial Control Systems* . Lexington.

Bisson, David. 2017. *Second Wave of Shamoon 2: Disttrack Can Now Wipe Organizations' VDI Snapshots.* 12 1. https://www.tripwire.com/state-of-security/security-data-protection/cyber-security/second-wave-shamoon-2-disttrack-can-now-wipe-organizations-vdi-snapshots/.

Bloomberg. 2016. *Editor's Picks.* 2016 September. http://www.chicagobusiness.com/article/20160923/NEWS07/160929874/trump-hotels-to-pay-50-000-fine-over-data-breaches.

Chipkin, Peter. 2009. *Bacnet for Field Technicians.* Vanvouver: Chipkin Automation.

—. 2010. *Modbus for Field Technicians.* Vancouver: Chipkin Automation.

CVE Details. 2016. *CVE Details The ultimate security vulnerability datasource.* 02 April. https://www.cvedetails.com/vulnerability-list/vendor_id-26/product_id-3436/version_id-92758/Microsoft-IIS-7.5.html.

2016. *CVE Details The ultimate security vulnerability datasource.* 2016 April. https://www.cvedetails.com/.

David E. Sanfer, Eric Schmitt. 2016. *Spy Agency Consesnus Grows That Russia Hacked D.N.C.* 26 July. http://www.nytimes.com/2016/07/27/us/politics/spy-agency-consensus-grows-that-russia-hacked-dnc.html?_r=0.

Drupal. 2016. *Drupal Core - Highly Critical - Public Service announcement - PSA-2014-003.* 02 April. https://www.drupal.org/PSA-2014-003.

DuckDuckGo.com. n.d. *Say hello to bangs.* Accessed June 26, 2017. https://duckduckgo.com/bang.

Durumeric, David Adrian and Karthikeyan Bhargavan and Zakir. 2015. "Imperfect Forward Secrecy: {H}ow {D}iffie-{H}ellman Fails." *22nd ACM Conference on Computer and Communications*, October.

Freifeld, Karen. 2016. *Trump Hotels settles with N.Y. Attorney General over data breaches.* 23 September. http://www.reuters.com/article/us-trumphotels-nyattorneygeneral-settlem-idUSKCN11T2KR.

2016. *https://censys.io/ipv4/*.* 18 September. https://censys.io/ipv4/*.

Hunt, Troy. 2012. *Shhh… don't let your response headers talk too loudly.* 28 February. Accessed November 2017, 5. https://www.troyhunt.com/shhh-dont-let-your-response-headers/.

ICIJ Database. n.d. *ICIJ Database.* Accessed December 20, 2016. https://offshoreleaks.icij.org/ .

n.d. *ILOVEYOU.* Accessed November 2017, 17. https://en.wikipedia.org/wiki/ILOVEYOU.

Knapp, Eric D, and Joel Thomas Langill. 2015. *Industrial Network Security, Securing Critical Infrastructure Networks for Smart Grid, SCADA, and Other Industrial Control Systems.* Waltham: Syngress.

Kubecka, Chrstina. n.d. "DefCon 22 Social Engineering CTF." HypaSec, *DefCon 22 Social Engineering CTF.* Las Vegas.

Matherly, John. 2016. *https://www.shodan.io/search?query=*.* 3 March. 2016.

Mehnle, Julian. 2016. *SPF Record Status.* 14 8. http://www.openspf.org/SPF_Record_Syntax.

2017. *Microsoft IIS.* 5 November. Accessed November 5, 2017. http://www.cvedetails.com/product/3436/Microsoft-IIS.html?vendor_id=26.

MITRE. 2016. *CVE Common Vulnerabilities and Exposures The Standard for Infromation Security Vulnerabilitiy Names.* 02 April . 2016.

National Institute of Standards and Technology. 2016. *Apache 2.2 vulneability search results.* 02 April. https://web.nvd.nist.gov/view/vuln/search-results?query=apache+2.2&search_type=all&cves=on.

Netcraft UK. 2016. *Site Report.* 2 April. https://www.netcraft.com.

NMap. n.d. *Home page.* Accessed May 1, 2016. Grabbing banners and naming services.

Offensive Security. 2016. *Offensive Security's Exploit Database Archive.* 02 April. https://www.exploit-db.com/.

OWASP. 2017. *Testing for Weak Encryption (OTG-CRYPST-004).* 17 July. Accessed August 22, 2018. https://www.owasp.org/index.php/Testing_for_Weak

Encryption(OTG-CRYPST-004).

Paganini, Pierluigi. 2017. *A Second variant of Shamoon 2 targets virtualization products* . 10 1. http://securityaffairs.co/wordpress/55235/malware/shamoon-2-virtualizations.html.

Rapid 7. 2016. *Rapid 7 Vulnerability & Exploit Database.* 02 April. https://www.rapid7.com/db/.

Rhysider, Jack. 2018. *Ep 13: Carna Botnet.* February 15. Accessed August 8, 2018. https://darknetdiaries.com/episode/13/ .

Roa, Ub Narasinga. 1994. "A Handbook of Kannada Proverbs, with English Equivalents." In *A Handbook of Kannada Proverbs, with English Equivalents*, by Ub Narasinga Roa, 5. New Delhi: Asian Educational Series.

Robtex.com. 2016. *Website Review.* 02 April. https://www.robtex.com.

Ruwhof, Sijmen. 2017. *How to hack the upcoming Dutch Elections* . 2 February. https://sijmen.ruwhof.net/weblog/1166-how-to-hack-the-upcoming-dutch-elections .

—. 2017. *How to Hack the Upcoming Dutch Elections.* 28 January. https://sijmen.ruwhof.net/weblog/1166-how-to-hack-the-upcoming-dutch-elections.

Spiderfoot. 2016. *SpiderFoot Documentation.* 20 September. http://www.spiderfoot.net/documentation/.

Time. 2016. *belgium-isis-nuclear-power-station-brussels.* 26 March. http://time.com/4271854/belgium-isis-nuclear-power-station-brussels/.

Tivārī, Gajendra. 1996. "Amana Prakāśana." In *Rañja līḍara ko bahuta hai*, by Gajendra Tivārī, 1. University of

California.

n.d. *View a List of HTTP Response Headers (IIS 7).* Accessed November 2017, 17. https://technet.microsoft.com/en-us/library/cc753686(v=ws.10).aspx.

13. *Weak Diffie-Hellman and the Logjam Attack.* 2015 October. Accessed June 2017, 7. https://weakdh.org.

Wikipedia. 2018. *ILOVEYOU.* 12 January. Accessed Februrary 20, 2018. ILOVEYOU.

—. 2017. *List of HTTP Status Codes.* 22 January . Accessed January 26, 2018. https://en.wikipedia.org/wiki/List_of_HTTP_status_codes#Unofficial_codes.

—. 2016. *Nmap.* 04 April. https://en.wikipedia.org/wiki/Nmap.

—. n.d. *NMap.* Accessed May 1, 2016. https://en.wikipedia.org/wiki/Nmap.

—. 2017. *Republican Party (United States).* 30 January. https://en.wikipedia.org/wiki/Republican_Party_(United_States) .

2017. *Wikipedia Saudi Aramco Cyber Attack.* 16 5. https://en.wikipedia.org/wiki/Saudi_Aramco#Cyber_Attack.

2017. *Wikipedia Saudi Aramco Cyber Attack.* 17 5. https://en.wikipedia.org/wiki/Saudi_Aramco#Cyber_Attack.

Wikipedia. 2016. *Wikipedia.* 19 September. https://en.wikipedia.org/wiki/Democratic_Party_(United_States).

—. 2016. *Wikipedia.* 13 March. https://en.wikipedia.org/wiki/Panama_Papers.

—. 2017. *Wikipedia.* 1 January. https://en.wikipedia.org/wiki/Campaigning_in_the_United_Kingdom_European_Union_membership_referendum,_2016#Grassroots_Out.

—. 2016. *Wikipedia.* 2 January. https://en.wikipedia.org/wiki/Fitna_(film).

Youtube.com. 2016. *Apache 2.2.15 exploit Youtube.com search results.* 02 April. https://www.youtube.com/results?q=apache+2.2.15+exploit.

Zakir Durumeric, David Adrian, Ariana Mirian, Michael Bailey, J. Alex Halderman. 2015. *A Search Engine Backed by {I}nternet-Wide Scanning.* Detriot: Proceedings of the 22nd ACM Conference on Computer and Communications Security.

Index

Who wrote this?

About the Author

Chris Kubecka, Security Researcher and CEO of HypaSec. HypaSec offers expert advice in cyber warfare, incident response management, lecturing, training in IT and ICS security, penetration testing, privacy and vulnerability scanning and writing services in security. HypaSec also build hands-on penetration and intelligence courses, such as a HypaSec hands-on version of the GIAC GPEN. Formerly, establishing several security groups for Saudi Aramco's international affiliates after the Shamon 1 attacks and headed the Information Protection Group for Aramco Overseas, Netherlands. Implementing and leading the Security Operations Centre, Network Operation Centre and Joint International Intelligence Group & the EU/UK Privacy Group for Aramco Overseas Company. With continuous professional experience in the field, her career includes the US Air Force, Space Command, private and public sector.

A conference presenter at Black Hat, OWASP, Security BSides, European Union Presidency for fintech and energy cyber security, CCC Chaos Computer Congress, Cyber Senate on ICS Security, Nuclear Cyber Security, European Council on Foreign Relations, OpenFest, Last H.O.P.E on water system insecurities and censorship, advises and lectures as an expert for several markets and governments. Chris has been featured in the media with Viceland News' Cyber Warfare series, Hacking the Infrastructure on HBO, Sky News, CNN, Fox News, Asian and European news outlets. Podcasts DarkNet Diaries and Security Weekly. MIT Technology Review "How to Implement Security after a Cyber Security Meltdown" March/April 2016 issue. Writing for 2600, Hackernoon, Free Code Camp, Peerlyst, several Bit Coin and defence related media.

Made in the USA
Coppell, TX
10 November 2026

11835562R00177